MAKING CRIME PAY

A Practical Guide to Mystery Writing

Stephanie Kay Bendel

A SPECTRUM BOOK

Prentice-Hall, Inc., Englewood Cliffs, New Jersey 07632

Library of Congress Cataloging in Publication Data

Bendel, Stephanie Kay.
   Making crime pay.

  "A Spectrum Book."
  Bibliography: p.
  Includes index.
   1. Detective and mystery stories—Technique.
I. Title.
PN3377.5.D4B4 1983   808.3'872   82-20426
ISBN 0-13-545939-7
ISBN 0-13-545921-4 (pbk.)

To Bill, Tim, and Joanna

A SPECTRUM BOOK.

Printed in the United States of America

10 9 8 7 6 5 4 3 2 1

ISBN 0-13-545939-7

ISBN 0-13-545921-4 (PBK.)

Cover design by Hal Siegel
Manufacturing buyer: Cathie Lenard

Prentice-Hall International, Inc., London
Prentice-Hall of Australia Pty. Limited, Sydney
Prentice-Hall Canada Inc., Toronto
Prentice-Hall of India Private Limited, New Delhi
Prentice-Hall of Japan, Inc., Tokyo
Prentice-Hall of Southeast Asia Pte. Ltd., Singapore
Whitehall Books Limited, Wellington, New Zealand
Editora Prentice-Hall do Brasil Ltda., Rio de Janeiro

Contents

Preface

This book is a practical guide for anyone involved in writing, teaching, or studying mystery or suspense fiction. It is written in a clear, informal manner and offers frequent examples to illustrate points being discussed.

It is a how-to book, written with an eye on the mystery reader. Those elements that specifically appeal to the readers of mysteries and the particular satisfactions that are derived from those elements are explained here in detail. Then special techniques for effectively developing them in a story are demonstrated with vivid examples.

Each chapter has been designed to cover as completely as possible one aspect of writing a mystery. Plotting, characterization, settings, viewpoint, style, tone, and such technical problems as handling flashbacks, dialogue, and tenses are explained with an emphasis on the parts they play in mystery fiction. Problems more specifically associated with mysteries—maintaining suspense, planting clues, directing suspicion fairly, and developing satisfying solutions—are discussed thoroughly.

If you've ever been curious about the inner workings of mystery fiction, here's the book that will explain it to you.

And if you've ever wanted to try your hand at writing a mystery, here's the book that will show you how!

ACKNOWLEDGMENTS

I gratefully wish to acknowledge the many hours of thoughtful evaluation of this material and helpful comments offered by Anne Perkins Dewey, Craig Shaw Gardner, and Charlotte M. Young.

Also, a special thanks to George P. McCrevan, Jr., for the extended use of personal reference material.

1

What Makes
Mysteries Different?

Ask any group of avid mystery fans to tell you exactly what they enjoy most about reading mysteries. Their answers will be quite predictable. You'll find that on the whole they fall into seven categories.

WHAT MYSTERY READERS LOOK FOR

1. *The enjoyment of being fooled.* Everyone likes to watch the magician saw the woman in half. No matter that we *know* it's an illusion and that the woman is in no danger whatsoever. There's a peculiar pleasure in knowing that what we *think* we see is not what is *really* happening.

A good mystery produces the same sort of enjoyment. All the clues are put in front of the readers. They *know* the answer is there, but they can't see it until the author is ready to reveal it.

2. *The pleasure of the puzzle.* It is one of the paradoxes of the genre that although mystery readers love to try to figure out the denouement, they are invariably disappointed if they succeed. If we see through the magician's illusion, we consider him a poor magician. If we can anticipate the ending,

it's not a good mystery. The pleasure is in the attempt to figure things out, not in the achievement.

Some mystery fans actually read with a notebook at hand. They jot down clues and make lists of suspects and motives as if they were personally charged with solving the crime at hand. No other genre offers the opportunity for such personal involvement on the part of the readers.

It is as if the magician calls us onto the stage and invites us to examine his equipment as closely as we like, defying us to understand how the illusion is produced. If there is pleasure in watching the magician at a distance, how much greater the pleasure in being fooled while standing at his side!

3. *Suspense.* Suspense is probably the most frequently given reason for reading mysteries. Exciting things are happening! Murders are committed under extraordinary circumstances. Lovely heroines are endangered. Villains are pursued. And the readers are invited to participate vicariously in all this excitement. It's a wonderful escape from everyday routine.

4. *Intriguing characters.* In real life, people who keep finding themselves in interesting situations tend to be interesting people. So must it also be in fiction, and mystery fiction has given the world plenty of colorful characters. Watching them interact, seeing them get into impossible situations, and trying to figure out how they will extricate themselves are part of the enjoyment of the mystery.

5. *The sense of unity.* Probably more than any other type of story, the mystery must be tightly plotted. Mystery readers expect a story with a beginning, a middle, and an end. They take great pleasure in watching the story unfold, knowing that all the elements presented will eventually fit neatly together.

6. *The sense of order.* In real life, justice doesn't often reign.

Crimes go unsolved. Criminals go free. Investigations have loose ends. Some questions are never answered. Mystery readers want to escape into a world in which chaos is resolved into order. No matter how bad things are in Chapter 3, the readers expect that by the end of the book the good guys will triumph and the bad guys will be punished.

7. *The thrill of sudden revelation.* Mystery readers live for those moments when they unexpectedly catch a glimpse of the truth. The big revelation, of course, comes at the end of the book, but a well-written mystery will provide lesser revelations along the way so that the readers cannot assume for long that they understand exactly what is going on.

In a good mystery, just at the point where the readers begin to feel that they are figuring things out, the author presents a new piece of information that changes everything. A new theory must be formulated.

There is a pleasurable sensation produced by these lesser revelations. It is similar to the experience of being on a Ferris wheel. The wheel has slowed, your seat is approaching the ramp, and you're sure the ride is over. Then suddenly, the wheel starts up again, you're thrown backward into your seat and whisked upward and around. You're off again!

Mystery readers *love* that feeling.

There are other reasons for reading mysteries, of course. But you will find these seven consistently given, no matter whether the readers are young or old, no matter what level of education they have attained, no matter what their social background may be.

You will find, too, that when you think about those mysteries you've enjoyed, the great ones provided all these satisfactions, and the good ones provided most of them.

Mysteries, you see, are not only good entertainment but a very special form of entertainment. If you are going to write them, it is good to know exactly what your readers will expect to find in your stories. Success, after all, is satisfying the customers!

It may seem like a large order to write a story that will provide the readers with all these satisfactions, but happily they tend to develop from the very elements of which a mystery is constructed. The author, however, must use those elements properly in order to achieve the desired effects.

THE ELEMENTS OF A MYSTERY

There are many types of mysteries, and over the years the borderlines of the genre have become blurred. In order to be of greatest benefit to aspiring writers, this book takes a broad view of what constitutes a mystery.

1. *The crime.* A mystery centers about a crime. Usually it must be a serious crime in order to keep the interest of the readers. Few people are willing to read three hundred pages to find out whether the hero solves a purse snatching.

Once we've selected a serious enough crime, we've got the opportunity to provide the escape and excitement the readers expect.

2. *Detection and pursuit.* A mystery involves the detection and/or the pursuit of a villain. In many cases the main question in the plot is "Who did it?" In others the villain may be known or strongly suspected from the beginning, and the question may be "How was it done?" or "Why was it done?" or "How can we prove this in a court of law?" In some cases, the main question may be "How can we physically catch the villain?"

Mysteries are made of questions. By asking these questions in interesting ways, we can provide the readers with a puzzle and a good deal of suspense. By answering them imaginatively, we'll provide the readers with the pleasure of being fooled and the sense of unity and the sense of order. And by asking and answering the questions in proper sequence, we can create sudden revelations.

3. *Suspense.* A mystery needs to have suspense maintained throughout. Even police procedurals cannot simply be the telling of routine police investigations, which, by and large, are dull and monotonous work, dealing mostly with colorless and unmysterious crimes. Suspense, as we shall see, involves anxiety, and that implies a personal involvement on the part of the readers. A mystery needs a protagonist whom the readers will care about and who faces a vital problem *involving the crime.* It's all right to have a romantic subplot (will the hero win the heroine's heart or won't he?), but the chief source of suspense must be in the solution of the crime.

4. *The puzzle.* A mystery needs a puzzle—or at least a crime with unusual features that place it outside the realm of everyday events. A man may shoot his wife, and the story probably won't rate more than a few lines in the local papers. But suppose the man is blind? Or suppose he's the state governor or an extraordinarily wealthy businessman? And what if he shot her with an antique flintlock that was stolen from a museum?

By putting unusual or incongruous details in our story, we can create a puzzle, intriguing characters, and an escape from reality for our readers.

5. *The plot.* A mystery needs a tight, believable plot. Every scene should move the story forward. That is, it should give the readers some information pertinent to the solution of the crime or describe events leading to the capture of the villain. Everything that happens should be a logical development that follows from the behavior and motivation of the characters. There should be no extra pieces, no missing pieces, and every piece of the puzzle should fit exactly.

Careful attention to detail in the construction of the plot results in the sense of unity and of order.

6. *Fair play.* A mystery demands fair treatment of the readers. Although mystery readers want to be fooled, they want to be fooled fairly. What does that mean? The principle can be illustrated by considering a couple of familiar riddles:

Q: What has four legs, weighs eight hundred pounds, is yellow, and sings?

A: Two four-hundred-pound canaries.

Although young children may appreciate this, mystery fans won't because the question contains false information. Canaries simply don't weigh four hundred pounds apiece, and there is no logical way to arrive at this answer.

On the other hand, mystery fans would appreciate the following:

Q: What has four wheels and flies?

A: A garbage truck.

Just as they're about to object that a garbage truck can't fly, the readers realize that *flies* can be a noun as well as a verb, and when the question is considered in that light, the answer makes sense! There was no false information given; the readers were allowed to mislead themselves. That's fair play!

And now that we have some idea of what goes into a good mystery, let's look at how to go about plotting one.

2
Plotting

Probably more than any other type of story, a mystery must have a tight plot. As we mentioned in Chapter 1, your readers want to experience a sense of unity—of everything fitting together, of having no unanswered questions at the end—and a sense of order—of inevitability, of rightness—that is found nowhere else but in a good mystery.

If you are going to provide those satisfactions, it stands to reason that your story will take some planning, and that's what plotting is.

A plot is a plan. It is concerned with the events in your story and with their sequence. A plot serves the same purpose that a blueprint does in the construction of a house. In much the same way that two homes may each have three bedrooms, two baths, a kitchen, a living room, and a dining room and still have entirely different floor plans, two works of fiction may concern themselves with the same events and still be entirely different stories.

To extend the analogy even further, two homes may have the same basic floor plan and still be very different because of the use of dissimilar materials in both the construction and the decor. Likewise, two works of fiction may have the same basic plot and yet be very different. Myths, legends, and popular folk tales are told and retold in many guises and are still enjoyed anew.

This means that you don't necessarily have to have a plot that no one has ever used before. In fact, many writers maintain that there are only a limited number of possible plots. What will make your story fresh will be your characters, their unique personalities, and the 101 details that only you could put into the story.

THE NECESSITY OF CONSTRUCTING A PLOT

Before you begin to construct anything, you need to know what the finished product will be like. Imagine a carpenter who finishes building a house only to discover that he has forgotten to put in a kitchen. At that point, he has two choices. He can tear apart a good portion of the building in order to integrate a kitchen into the existing floor plan. This, of course, would be expensive and time-consuming. His alternative is to tack a kitchen onto one end of the building. That, however, will result in a house that will be inconvenient, unattractive, and hard to sell.

Writers who don't give much thought to plotting find themselves in a similar situation. They produce stories with something missing. And if they are fortunate enough to figure out what they've done wrong, they're faced with extensive rewriting in order to produce a salable product.

On the other hand, writers who are conscious of the requirements of a good plot usually end up with the right things in the right places.

THE REQUIREMENTS OF A GOOD PLOT

Every story concerns a problem. Essentially we read a story to watch a character solve a problem. But it isn't quite that simple. In a good story:

1. The main character must be interesting.
2. The problem he deals with must be interesting.
3. The solution to the problem must be satisfying.

What do these requirements mean? Let's look at them more closely and, in particular, see how they pertain to the writing of a mystery.

The Main Character Must Be Interesting

All readers of fiction are looking for vicarious experiences. They want to feel that they have lived through the events you are describing. One way you can provide this feeling to your readers is to get them to identify as closely as possible with your protagonist.

The creation of the protagonist will be discussed thoroughly in Chapter 5, so we'll not say too much on the matter here, except for one point that has as much to do with plot as with characterization: The readers must *care* what happens to the protagonist.

Imagine that our hero, Ben, is a rookie policeman working on his first big case: the brutal murders of several young women. There is evidence that the killer stalks his victims for some time before he strikes.

Our hero is one of a hundred police officers working or the case. Every lead is being tracked down, every possible clue investigated. Every available bit of technology is being employed.

Pause a moment and ask yourself how the readers will feel at this point. Will they want to continue reading to find out what happens to Ben? Why *should* they? Ben is indistinguishable from the other ninety-nine officers on the case.

Let's rewrite the scenario to *isolate* our hero and make him *vulnerable*. Vulnerability may be physical—that is, the character is in danger of losing his life—or emotional—that is, the character is in danger of losing something or someone he cares deeply about.

Suppose an arrest has been made in this case. The authorities are convinced that they have the killer, and the general investigation has been discontinued. The police officers have been reassigned to other cases. Ben, however, has the nagging feeling that they have the wrong man and that the real killer is still free.

But he has no proof. The reasons for his beliefs are largely intuitive. Thus, no one will listen to him and he's ordered to work on a relatively unimportant investigation. When Ben's friend, Karen, tells him that she's convinced someone is watching her, Ben fears that she is to be the next victim. But he can't convince his superiors.

It's up to Ben to catch the killer—and he'll have to do it *alone*.

See what has happened? We've isolated Ben from the other police officers and given him something to lose. We've made Ben—and the problem—far more interesting.

Remember that isolation and vulnerability demand that the protagonist have as little emotional and technical support as possible in facing the problem.

Suppose Marcia, who's receiving death threats in the mail, has a large caring family who gathers around her. Someone is always with her. Sophisticated alarms have been installed in her house and police officers and trained dogs are patrolling the neighborhood.

The readers aren't being asked to worry very much about Marcia.

But suppose Marcia has no family or that she's far from home and without the means to install alarms or hire a bodyguard. The police—for one reason or another—don't take the threats seriously. They won't help her either.

Now the readers are being invited to worry a great deal about Marcia. She's isolated and vulnerable.

There is, as always, an exception to the foregoing. Suppose you are writing a story in which the protagonist is an antihero: Bruno is a master criminal who is planning to commit a terrible crime. Now you want the readers to be afraid that the protagonist *will* succeed, so you have to make success look inevitable. You can give him all the friends and technological help you like. And, of course, he will fail in spite of it.

Whether your protagonist is good or evil or somewhere in between, the point is that the readers must *care* what happens to him or her.

The Problem Must Be Interesting

Quite naturally, in a mystery or suspense novel, the main problem will center about a crime. But that in itself is not enough to make it interesting.

Rowena is visiting her fifth cousin Thelma, who tells her that three years ago someone stole her teapot. It wasn't worth much, but it was kind of cute and Thelma always wondered who took it and why. Curious, Rowena decides to figure out what happened.

How long do you think you could keep your readers interested in this problem?

How do you determine whether or not a problem will be interesting to the readers? In general, it must be:

1. important
2. personal
3. urgent
4. apparently impossible to solve

Let's consider these points in turn.

The problem must be important. Although a short story may successfully deal with lesser crimes, it is hard to keep a reader in suspense for a couple of hundred pages if the protagonist's problem is relatively small—say, a series of housebreaks or a run-of-the-mill bank robbery. Most mystery novels require a murder to keep up reader interest.

Suspense novels, on the other hand, can succeed without a murder, *providing the crime is big enough.* The theft of ten thousand dollars won't hold the readers for long. The theft of ten million probably will. The theft of a hundred million certainly will.

By the same token, the readers won't care about the theft of a diamond necklace from a woman who owns a dozen others. But make that necklace unique, of historical significance, and priceless, and the readers will care.

The problem must be personal. Sometimes even a murder won't seem very important to the readers. If the victim is a stranger and his death is of no particular importance to the protagonist or anyone he cares about, the problem becomes abstract. If the protagonist isn't personally affected—either by being physically endangered or emotionally involved—it won't make much difference to him (or to the readers) whether or not the problem is solved. The protagonist must stand to lose something important.

The problem must be urgent. No matter how great a problem you have, it won't generate much anxiety if you have all the time in the world to solve it. Your plot should impose some sort of deadline on the protagonist. If the killer isn't caught, he'll kill again. Or he'll get away. Or an innocent person will be punished for the crime.

Sometimes the urgency is of a personal nature: the need to know how or why a friend or relative died. Or the need to avenge a particularly wrongful death by seeing justice done. *Curiosity, of itself, is not enough.* If your detective comes upon an odd murder and investigates simply to satisfy his curiosity, the readers will not feel a sense of urgency.

The problem must appear impossible to solve. There's no satisfaction in solving an easy problem. And it's no fun watching someone else do it, either.

What your readers want is for you to show them a problem that looks as if it can't be solved—and then show them your protagonist solving it.

This doesn't mean that the protagonist must be totally overwhelmed by the problem from Chapter 1 on. The readers also find it satisfying if, each time the protagonist takes steps to solve the problem, it becomes worse or more complex.

What you are doing here is playing a kind of game with your readers. You present a problem to them and try to anticipate every solution to that problem that they will think of. Then you show them that none of their solutions will work. And then—when the situation seems hopeless to the readers—you solve the problem. And you do it in a way that your readers aren't likely to have thought of.

Remember Marcia, the young woman who was receiving

death threats? We've already said that she has no family around, the police won't help her, and she hasn't the means to hire protection.

What will the readers think of as possible solutions to the problem? Get a ferocious watchdog? Let her do it and have someone poison the dog. Buy a gun? Let her try it and find out that there's a waiting period to buy firearms in this state. Ask a neighbor—even if she hardly knows the neighbors—for help? Let her find out that someone has spread the rumor that Marcia is a witch and the neighbors will have nothing to do with her. Pack up and leave? Go anywhere? Let her try—and find that someone has slashed the tires on her car. And the only garage in the area which sells tires is closed for the weekend.

Now what? Why, make the situation even worse! It's getting dark, the phone's gone dead. The lights go out. And there's someone moving around outside.

Now let Marcia get herself out of this!

Remember, the more obstacles in the protagonist's way, the more difficult it is to solve the problem, the more interested your readers will be in watching her do it.

The Solution Must Be Satisfying

It is not enough to get your protagonist in deep trouble and out again. When the problem is finally solved, it must be done in a satisfying way. This means that the solution comes about *in a logical manner*, not through coincidence or happy accident. The solution must also come about *through the actions of the protagonist*. No one else can come to the rescue at the last moment—unless, of course, the protagonist has found some brilliant and unorthodox way to summon help.

Marcia's old friend Patrick can't simply decide to pay

her a surprise visit and drop in just in time to rescue her. Nor can the attacker suffer a ruptured appendix or get struck by lightning, thus allowing Marcia to escape.

It is true that fortunate coincidences sometimes occur in real life, and crimes are sometimes solved by accident. But when such things happen in a story, the readers will feel frustrated and dissatisfied. They want the protagonist to do the work.

Marcia has to get out of that mess all by herself.

Two other things should be said about the solution of the problem: First, *it should coincide as nearly as possible with the climax of the story.* Action and tension should be a maximum levels. Thus, it helps if your solution can be revealed under spine-tingling circumstances. A death-defying chase, for example, or a deadly confrontation with the killer. In general, the scene in which all the characters are called together so that the hero can reveal the identity of the villain and explain how he deduced it is considered passé. If you must resort to a scene of this kind, remember that the tension level will necessarily be low: The killer cannot reasonably be expected to get away from a roomful of people once his or her identity has been revealed. You'll want to compensate for this deficiency as best you can. In general, the scene ought to be as short and dramatic as possible.

Also, *the readers should not be able to anticipate the solution.* It is a basic tenent of fiction writing in general that what happens must seem inevitable. That is doubly true for mystery writing. The readers want to feel that the solution of the mystery is a perfectly logical result of all that has gone before—that they *should* have seen it. But they don't want to be able to anticipate it. The ending must be a surprise and yet not a surprise.

Later in this book we'll discuss some methods for keeping the solution from being obvious while at the same time making it seem inevitable.

HOW TO PLOT

Now that we know what we want to end up with—an interesting character and an interesting problem with a satisfying solution—where do we begin?

There is no single right way to develop a plot. Different writers have different methods. Some begin with one or more characters, others with an idea or two. Some begin with the ending or a setting or a title or a combination of these things. The important thing is not what you begin with but what you end up with.

Briefly, we'll outline these different methods of plotting. You might like to experiment, trying to develop a plot using various methods, and decide which works best for you in general. You may also find that if you are having difficulty with a plot, it may be helpful to try developing it by a different method.

Methods of Plotting

1. *Developing the character first.* This is often the preferred method of initiating a series character. The idea is that if you know your protagonist thoroughly, you can put him or her in different situations and be pretty certain what will happen. However, this method can just as well be used for a single piece of fiction. Let's see how it works.

Suppose we'd like to create a female private eye. We'd like her to be tough enough to handle the rough characters she comes up against yet attractive enough in an obviously feminine way that we can develop a romantic subplot.

How did she become a private eye? Perhaps she was married to one who owned his own agency and had a number of operatives working for him. She helped him with his cases and thus learned the detective business. Then the husband was killed. For financial reasons our heroine was forced to take over the business. Suddenly she had to be aggressive, to summon all her inner strength in order to be the boss of an established detective agency. Yet she's a vulnerable woman who is lonely and who misses her husband.

We need to give her a name that reflects this duality—a name that is attractively feminine and yet reflects her ability to take care of herself. How about Nicole? We can call her Nikki must of the time.

If we were actually developing this character for a novel, we would do a lot more groundwork at this point, giving her a complete background and a well-developed and interesting personality. Some methods for doing this will be discussed in Chapters 4 and 5. For the purposes of this example, however, we'll assume that the groundwork has been done.

The next step is to give Nikki a problem. Suppose Cully, one of her operatives, is found dead under suspicious circumstances. The police rule it a suicide, but Nikki finds that hard to believe. She's known Cully for years, and she never saw any indication that he was suicidal. Furthermore, she knows his family, and the suicide ruling is causing them great distress.

The circumstances of Cully's death were such that it couldn't have been an accident. Murder is the only other explanation. But no one seems to have a motive for murdering Cully.

At this point, let's stop and evaluate our problem in order to make sure it's interesting enough. Is it important? Because it deals with a suspicious death, yes. Is it personal? Yes, because Nikki knew Cully well. Is it urgent? This is one of these cases where the urgency arises from the personal element. When someone you know dies suddenly under questionable circumstances, there is a very real need to know what happened and why. However, we could still beef this point up a bit.

Suppose Nikki recalls a chance remark Cully made shortly before his death. In retrospect the remark leads Nikki to suspect that Cully may have been killed because of his work for her agency. Now Nikki feels responsible and we've increased both the urgency and the personal element of the problem.

Is the problem apparently impossible to solve? At this point we can't really tell. If Cully's remark was suitably vague and offhand—just enough to indicate that there was something odd about his current investigation but not enough to give Nikki an obvious idea of what he meant—we're off to a good start. As the story moves along, we'll place greater and greater obstacles in Nikki's way so that it will seem more and more difficult to find out what happened to Cully.

Where do we go from here? We can either develop the other characters and then figure out who killed Cully and why, or we can figure out what happened to Cully and then develop the characters who did it.

Another version of plotting that begins with characterization is that in which you develop all your major characters thoroughly and then create a situation in which two or more of them are in conflict.

Suppose Damien is a successful banker who has always handled his personal finances conservatively. He abhors unnecessary debts and frivolous expenditures. His wife, Greta, has always been content with their life-style, secure in the knowledge that she has done much better in her marriage than her sister, Lisa, did in hers.

But when Lisa divorces her husband and marries a multimillionaire who lives lavishly, Greta starts pressing Damien for a more exciting life-style—one that is beyond their financial reach.

Can you see how a murder might result from this situation?

2. *Beginning with an idea.* Have you ever heard of a negative hallucination? Hallucinating is seeing something that is not physically present. Negatively hallucinating is *not* seeing something which *is* physically present. It occurs in rare instances when the sight of an object or a person would create severe psychological stress in a subject. The subject must be someone who habitually copes with problems by denying their existence. If this ability to deny reality is developed to a great enough degree, the subject can become selectively blind.

For example, Cecil has had a morbid fear of peanuts since his mother choked to death on one in his presence. If Cecil is a strong denier, he can sit at a bar and not see the dish of peanuts at his elbow. And if the person on the next barstool says, "Pass the peanuts," Cecil will say in all sincerity, "What peanuts?".

And if Cecil is the rare person whose denial capability is nearly total, the bartender can drop the peanuts, one by one, into Cecil's hand and Cecil may *feel* them and perhaps *hear* them striking the bar as they fall out of his hand. But his eyes will tell him that *nothing is there!*

Can you imagine what a terrifying experience that could be?

Suppose we wanted to use the concept of negative hallucination in a mystery story. What if Heather witnesses Ned's murder and experiences selective blindness? What is it she doesn't want to see? The weapon? No good. It's too easy to tell from the autopsy what the weapon must have been. What about the identity of the murderer?

Why does she want to deny the murderer's identity? What if the killer is Oliver, the man she loves? Perhaps we should go one step better: What if the killer *looks like Oliver*? In fact, let's say the killer is trying to frame Oliver and has arranged things so that Heather will see the murder committed in hopes that her eyewitness testimony will convict Oliver.

But instead Heather swears that she saw the poker fly through the air and bash in Ned's skull all by itself! Or perhaps she insists that a ghost killed Ned because immediately afterward an invisible force shoved her back against the doorjamb and *something* rushed past her! Or maybe she testifies that she saw Ned killed by a man without a face!

Because she's telling what she honestly believes to be the truth, she may even pass a lie detector test. This will indeed be a nice (and apparently impossible) problem for our detective to solve!

Sooner or later, of course, we'll have to educate our readers on the subject of negative hallucinations, and someone will have to suggest hypnotizing Heather to find out what she really saw (for her subconscious mind knows). But then—and here's a nice twist—Heather will tell the police that she saw *Oliver* kill Ned, and suspicion will still be directed away from the killer.

We must remember to show the readers that Heather is the type of person who is constantly denying unpleasant realities so that when we've explained the concept of negative hallucinations, the readers will easily accept her as a person capable of them.

It would probably be good to make Oliver a perfectly lovable fellow so that the readers will really be thrown when Heather admits that she saw him commit the murder. The readers will then experience great satisfaction when Oliver is finally cleared.

We'll also have to figure out who the murderer is and why he wanted to kill Ned and frame Oliver for it. And how does he manage to look so much like Oliver? And who else is in this story and what roles will they play?

In general, plotting consists of asking questions and then answering them. *It is often useful to reject the first answer that comes to mind.* Doing this keeps the plot from being too simple. After all, if that answer is the first one that occurred to you, chances are good that it'll occur to a lot of your readers as well.

3. *Beginning at the end.* Again, we are going to ask questions and then answer them. But instead of asking "What happens next?" we'll ask "What *has* happened?"

There are two versions of this method. One is to imagine the most terrifying circumstances that you can. This will be the climax of your story.

Suppose Annette is in the hospital for minor surgery. She's been heavily sedated and is lying on a gurney waiting to be taken to the operating room. Instead, the orderly takes her into the freight elevator. He pulls an empty syringe from his pocket. Annette, who is barely conscious, knows that an injection of air into a major blood vessel can because a fatal embolism.

Who is the orderly? Why does he want to kill Annette? How is she going to get out of this?

Your questions are ready-made. Your story is limited only by your imagination in coming up with the answers.

In the other version of beginning-at-the-end plotting, you start with the key fact—that bit of knowledge that will resolve the mystery.

For example, it is possible to tell the approximate age of a scar. Thus, you could tell the difference between a scar that's twenty years old and one that's only five years old.

Now you start asking questions: Why would anyone lie about the age of a scar? To hide a true identity or protect a false one? To hide the circumstances under which the scar was formed? What *really* happened?

Again, your story is limited only by your imagination.

4. *Beginning with a setting.* Some stories could only happen at a certain time and/or place. Sherlock Holmes's forays into forensic science were interesting because evidence wasn't

commonly examined in a scientific manner in the late nineteenth and early twentieth century. Today, Holmes's laboratory experiments would be pathetically inadequate for criminal investigations. Doyle's stories are inseparable from the *time* in which they are set.

On the other hand, stories such as Robin Cook's *Coma* and Mary Higgins Clark's *The Cradle Must Fall* couldn't have been written without using a hospital setting. In other words, these stories are inseparable from the *place* in which they are set.

If you want to set a story in a certain time or place, ask yourself, "What happens here that can't (or won't) happen anywhere else?" or "How was daily life different in this particular time period?"

Suppose your story begins in San Francisco on V-J Day in 1945. Sailors are everywhere. Strangers are kissing and dancing in the streets. Little impromptu parties are taking place all over the city. Liquor is flowing, car horns are honking, everyone is talking, laughing, and crying at once.

All kinds of unusual things could happen under these circumstances. A man might walk right through a crowded hotel lobby without being noticed or remembered by anyone. A woman's screams might not be heard or, if they are, might be ignored. The hotel rooms might not get cleaned at the usual time. No one would pay attention when dinner reservations aren't kept. And suppose the next morning you needed an alibi and you realized you hadn't the faintest idea how to find the people you were with last night? In fact, you didn't know who they were?

A setting will evoke certain characters with particular temperaments, moods, and responses. Suppose, for example, you have a basic plot for a mystery that requires your setting to be one in which a group of men are confined with little contact with the outside world. You could set your story in a research base in Antarctica, a federal prison in California, or a monastery in France. In each case you'll have different characters and your stories will be very different.

In the same way, a story about the killing of a singer in Las Vegas will be very different from one about the murder of a soprano at the Met. And a murder aboard a fishing trawler will produce a different story from one aboard a luxury yacht.

When you begin plotting a story from the setting, try to capture the moods and feelings that people have in that place. Ask yourself what kind of people are there. Why are they there? How are they different from other people? What is the history of the place and how does it affect the people there now? How do these people feel? What do they like, dislike, hope, or fear?

As you answer your questions, characters and plot ideas should begin to take shape in your mind. Keep asking questions and answering them until you've got the essential ingredients of a good plot: an interesting character and an interesting problem with a satisfying solution.

3

Thickening the Plot

In Chapter 1 we listed seven things readers look for in a mystery:

1. The enjoyment of being fooled
2. The pleasure of the puzzle
3. Suspense
4. Intriguing characters
5. A sense of unity
6. A sense of order
7. The thrill of sudden revelation

If you stop to think about it, four of these elements—the enjoyment of being fooled, the pleasure of the puzzle, suspense, and the thrill of sudden revelation—depend on the author's ability to keep the reader from anticipating how things are going to turn out.

Thus, one of your major concerns in plotting a mystery is to make sure that your story is complex enough to be satisfying. At the same time, everything that occurs in the story must be perfectly logical (even though it may not seem so at the time). If your readers come to the end of your story saying to themselves, "But Caroline *couldn't* have known where to look for the missing icepick until *after* she'd read Miranda's diary," their sense of order will be offended and your story won't satisfy them.

Your obligation to play fair with your readers goes even further: You cannot withhold information merely for the purpose of keeping the readers in the dark. Information withheld must be logically withheld. Similarly, false information must be logically falsified.

At first glance, it would seem that these restrictions require you to make the truth so obvious to the readers that they would easily be able to anticipate the ending.

How do you complicate the plot and still keep everything logical? How do you obscure the truth and do it fairly? Here are a few good methods:

DEVELOPING SUBPLOTS

It is a lot more difficult to solve two problems at the same time than it is to solve them one at a time. The elements of one problem intrude upon the elements of the other. You are distracted and sometimes forced to make difficult decisions.

Life is like that. Your boss wants that final report on his desk in the morning and you're coming down with a bad cold. On top of that, your car won't start. One way or another, we all go through life juggling problems.

Unless you are writing a very short story, you can use this fact to your advantage and develop subplots to make your story more complex. There's nothing mysterious about creating subplots; you are simply telling more than one story at a time. The stories are related because they involve some of the same characters and they happen during the same period of time.

One method of developing a subplot is to *give the protagonist more than one problem to deal with.*

Plot. Matt is investigating a huge stock swindle. One man has already been murdered and a business that is the lifeblood of Matt's best friend stands on the verge of ruin if the swindler isn't caught soon.

Subplot. Matt has loved Lucy from afar for some time, but Lucy's wealthy family doesn't consider him a suitable match for her. Lucy is especially devoted to her terminally ill father, Sidney, and would never go against his wishes. Matt is trying to win Sidney's approval.

The plot and the subplot are related because they both concern problems Matt has to deal with. However, they are not closely related, since Matt is the only common factor in both plot and subplot.

In general, a story is stronger if the plot and subplot (or subplots) are intertwined as closely as possible.

How could we make this story tighter? As things stand, Matt hopes to solve both his problems. What if we set things up so that it seems he can't possibly do that? What if Matt discovers that Sidney probably directed the stock swindle?

If Matt exposes Sidney, Lucy will never forgive him for forcing her father to die in disgrace. But if Sidney isn't exposed, Matt's best friend will lose millions and see his life's work destroyed.

Now we've knotted the two story lines pretty nicely. When Matt catches Lucy trying to destroy some of her father's business records, he can't be sure (and, of course, neither can the readers) whether she's obeying her father's orders blindly or whether she knows about the swindle and is trying to protect him. Or maybe she was in on the swindle from the beginning.

We've created several logical possibilities.

Another method for generating subplots is to *give more than one character a serious problem*.

In fact, it's a good idea to give every halfway important character some kind of a problem. If the problem is reasonably serious and the character resolves it by the end of the story, it serves as a subplot. If the problem isn't that serious or if it isn't resolved, it will still help to characterize the person or persons who must deal with it.

Suppose that our protagonist, Randall, discovers that the art treasures he inherited upon the recent death of his father are fakes. He had hoped to sell them to a museum and use the money to rescue his business from bankruptcy. When Randall tries to figure out what happened to the real art treasures, he learns that his father had suspected the substitution. Randall then realizes that his father's death was not entirely natural. He calls in the police to investigate.

Randall's wife, Carrie, disappointed in the loss of the badly needed money, is drinking more than ever. She's been seeing a psychiatrist who specializes in the treatment of alcoholics and she has fallen in love with him.

Randall's son, Terrence, is fifteen and has been feeling emotionally neglected because of his parents' preoccupation with their problems. Terrence turned to drugs and is now breaking into houses in order to support his habit. When the police are called in to investigate his grandfather's death, Terrence fears that they will discover his own illegal activities. He temporarily tries to do without the drugs he is accustomed to, but he becomes ill and despondent.

Randall's young cousin Moira, who had been his father's live-in nurse, inherited almost nothing and now faces an uncertain future. She knows about Carrie's affair and Terrence's drug problems.

Here are four people with problems and the people and the problems are related. If the main plot deals with discovering who stole the art treasures and killed Randall's father, some subplots might be:

1. Will Randall lose his business and/or his wife?
2. Will Carrie overcome her drinking problem?
3. Will Terrence become more deeply involved in drugs and crime, straighten out, be caught, or commit suicide?
4. What will Moira do about her financial plight?

This opens up all kinds of possibilities in our story. If Moira is discovered to have deposited a sizable sum into her bank account, it may be that she stole the art treasures in the first place. On the other hand, she could be blackmailing Terrence or Carrie.

• OBSCURING THE TRUTH AND DOING IT FAIRLY

Developing subplots is only one way to obscure the truth without unfairly deceiving the reader. Here are some others.

Offering Different Interpretations of the Facts

Suppose Uncle Abner has been murdered. Colette, the maid, tells the police inspector that she heard Abner and his nephew Tom shouting at each other in Abner's room shortly before the murder must have taken place. She couldn't understand most of what they were shouting about, for the door was closed. But she is certain about one thing: Abner had shouted very deliberately, "Get out of here!" Furthermore, when Tom came down the stairs a few moments later, he was flushed and perspiring and Colette concluded that he was very angry.

At this point the readers will have to regard Tom with some suspicion, particularly if he stands to gain by Abner's death.

But suppose we later hear Tom's version of what happened: He'd gone to Abner's room to discuss an unimportant matter and had had to raise his voice because Abner wasn't wearing his hearing aid. As Tom tried to talk to him, the old man became more and more frustrated, finally shouting that he'd dropped his hearing aid that morning and it had disappeared under his massive bed. "*Get* it *out!* I can't *hear!*" he'd shouted at Tom. Because the huge bed was hard to move on the thick carpet, Tom had to squeeze under the bed to reach the hearing aid and, being a large person, he'd had quite a struggle. Thus, his face was red and he was perspiring when he left the room shortly afterward.

Now the readers will have to decide what they think happened, for it isn't at all clear. But we have not misled them. Tom and Colette may both be telling the truth as they see it. And even if Tom is lying, he is doing so logically, trying to give an innocuous explanation for what Colette saw and heard.

Placing Two Significant
but Unrelated Events Close Together

Here is another method of handling information that invites the readers to mislead themselves.

Suppose that Inspector Wilson overhears Marta and her husband, Stephen, quarreling bitterly at a cocktail party. The next morning Wilson learns that Marta has been murdered in her bedroom. The house has been broken into, apparently by a man wearing size-11 shoes, and several items of value are missing.

Stephen, who wears size-9 shoes, says he spent the night at his club because he and Marta had quarreled. Inspector

Wilson learns that it would be difficult—but not impossible— for Stephen to have left and returned to the club during the night without being seen. And, of course, Stephen has no way of proving he didn't do just that.

Consider: Everything Stephen has said and done is consistent with his innocence. Yet most readers will be reluctant to believe him completely. They will want to assume that there is *some* connection between the quarrel and Marta's death. Until he's completely cleared, Stephen will remain a suspect in the readers' minds.

Involving Your Readers Emotionally

Remember that your readers' judgments are at least partly emotional. If they like a character, they'll be reluctant to suspect him or her seriously, in spite of the evidence. They'll also place more suspicion than logic alone would warrant upon a person they don't like.

Thus, although the only evidence against Stephen is circumstantial, if he loses his temper over nothing, is unkind to a dog, tells an unnecessary lie, or crows over the fact that the waitress in the restaurant undercharged him, he'll be regarded with increasing suspicion.

On the other hand, we may introduce Stephen's neighbor, Brandon, who wears size-11 shoes and who desperately needs money. Brandon can't prove he was asleep at the time of Marta's death, but if we make him charming and friendly, thoughtful and witty, our readers will resist suspecting him.

Giving Several People Something to Hide

This is another useful device for obscuring the truth. If several people have something to hide, they will logically lie to cover it up. The lies, however, make it more difficult to figure out what really happened. They also direct suspicion toward the liars at various times.

Surprising the Readers Now and Then

Have you ever been reading a mystery and had the feeling that you knew where the story was going, and then— wham!—something totally unexpected happened? Suddenly you weren't at all sure how the story would turn out.

Mystery readers like surprises such as this, and you, as the author, should consciously try to provide them with a few.

Often, such surprises come about simply as a result of giving the readers information in a certain sequence.

If Archie is going to be murdered in Chapter 2 and Ron is going to be murdered in Chapter 10 and if Ron is going to be the chief suspect in Archie's murder sometime between Chapters 2 and 10, why not have Ron killed when suspicion against him is at a peak? That way, his death raises a new question (if he didn't do it, who *did?*) and changes the way the readers must view events.

In contrast, if we kill Ron after he's been cleared of suspicion, the readers will experience far less surprise and may not have to change their theories as to the real killer's identity.

Sometimes the method in which information is obtained can be surprising.

If Eleanor is to discover that she is an adoptee, she could find it out from Aunt Hester, who comes to her one morning and says, "Sit down, Eleanor. I have something to tell you."

Or a stranger could show up on her doorstep and inform her that she is an heir to the estate of her grandmother—a grandmother she didn't know she had. Or that she is now the legal guardian of a younger brother she didn't know she had.

Obviously, Eleanor is going to be surprised whether she learns of the adoption from Aunt Hester or from the stranger, but the stranger gives her the information in a more effective way.

Beware of contrived surprises, however. No matter how unexpected the event may be, in retrospect it must be a logical outgrowth of what has gone before.

PLAUSIBILITY

No matter how much you work at developing your plot, it will not be successful if at any point your readers find it implausible.

Plausibility and possibility are not the same thing. Just because you know someone who can walk a tightrope blindfolded with his hands tied behind his back doesn't mean that your readers will believe that your hero can do it to get out of a tight spot.

Problems with plausibility arise in different ways.

1. *Stereotypes and clichés.* Resist the temptation to make all your blondes beautiful and dumb. Don't make all your police officers Irish or all your laundrymen Chinese. Your readers have seen these types so often that they no longer seem like real people, and you would have to work twice as hard as usual to make your characters come alive.

By the same token, beware of having your characters talk and act in ways that are too familiar. If the lovely damsel throws her arms around your protagonist's neck and murmurs, "My hero!" and her father says, "I like your style, son. How would you like a vice-presidency in my company?" your readers will only groan instead of being thrilled that things have turned out so well. They've seen all this before, and it no longer interests them.

If, on the other hand, the damsel throws her arms around the hero, kisses him and murmurs, "You bastard!" and her father grins and says, "I know you saved my daughter's life, but I'm still going to sue the hell out of you, Benson!" your readers are far more likely to feel satisfied.

2. *Fortunate coincidences.* Beware of having anything in your story "just happen." If it doesn't normally occur that way in real life, your readers will feel—and rightly so—that you are forcing things to happen just to make your story work out.

If your heroine needs a piece of rope to lower herself out of the window of the bedroom in which she's being held prisoner and she "just happens" to find some rope at the back of the bedroom closet, your readers won't believe it. And it doesn't matter if you know a dozen people who keep rope in their closets!

3. *Hunches and lucky guesses.* Whenever a character possesses some special knowledge or information, he or she must obtain it in a plausible manner. This applies to hunches and guesses, too.

Suppose your hero needs to get into his boss's safe surreptitiously. On a hunch, he tries a combination corresponding to the date of the boss's wife's birthday and the door swings open. Not only won't your readers believe this, but they'll be distracted wondering how he knew the boss's wife's birthdate.

It is true that in real life people sometimes have hunches that turn out to be correct, but usually such hunches are based on some pattern or prior knowledge that points to a likely solution to the problem at hand.

For example, suppose we—and our hero—already know that his boss tends to select numerical combinations which are connected with his wife in some way. Perhaps we know that his license plate number corresponds to the last six digits in her social security number and that he specially requested a telephone number in which the last four digits correspond to the date of their wedding. Now, when our hero surmises that the safe combination could be the same as the wife's birthdate, it isn't just a lucky guess—it's a logical possibility, and the readers will appreciate that. Don't forget, however, that we still have to explain how the hero knew the boss's wife's birthdate!

4. *Obvious oversights.* In any given situation, there are certain things that the average person would think to do. You cannot allow your characters to overlook obvious solutions to their problems.

If your hero is locked in a room and he sees that the key is in the keyhole on the other side of the door, he's got to think of slipping a piece of paper under the door and pushing the key out with a pencil and pulling the paper and the key under the door. Too many of your readers know this trick for your hero to overlook it. If he does, your readers will wonder—in exasperation—why. If you show them that he doesn't have a piece of paper, however, or that his pencil is too thick to work into the keyhole, then you can let him find another way to get out.

Similarly, if your heroine sees a prowler outside her house late at night, she has *got* to call the police. Or try to.

If the police don't believe her—for some logical reason—or if it's a small town and the only officer available is tied up with a serious emergency, she's got to try to call a friend or neighbor. If she's new in town and doesn't have any friends yet and she doesn't know the names of her neighbors, or if the phone doesn't work—because the prowler has cut the line—*then* you are justified in leaving her to cope with her problem alone.

5. *Extraordinary abilities.* You may wish to endow your protagonist with some special ability—say she's a crack shot or he's got a black belt in karate.

The important thing to remember in this case is that you cannot simply pull this ability out of thin air. You must let your readers know about any special talent *before it is called into use*.

If, in Chapter 1, we show our heroine shooting bullseyes on the target range, our readers will accept it when she expertly shoots the villain without harming the child he's holding hostage in Chapter 20.

If the readers see our hero in his karate uniform or hear him canceling his martial arts class early in the story, they'll be very satisfied when he decks the villain with a well-executed chop to the neck.

6. *Technical facts and procedures.* Because of the tremendous recent growth in communications and the mass media, today's average reader is exposed to more information than ever before. This imposes a greater burden on the author to make sure that the facts presented are accurate.

If your FBI agent dusts the ransom note for fingerprints, most of your readers will wonder where this fellow was during his investigative training. They'll know that chemical treatment is routinely used to bring out fingerprints from paper. They've seen it on television. Some of them will even know that iodine fumes or solutions of either ninhydrin or silver nitrate are used, so if you're going to mention chemicals, you had better know that, too.

And don't limit your accuracy on technical details only to matters of investigation. Your readers are sophisticated enough to know that your character can't get into someone else's safe deposit box simply by stealing the key. Nor is your villain likely to get past the bank's alarms merely by cutting off the electricity.

Remember that the business of writing fiction is creating an imaginary world. The more this fictional world conforms to the world with which the readers are familiar, the more readily they will accept it.

Thicken your plot, by all means, but thicken it plausibly!

4

Creating Three-Dimensional Characters

A story cannot exist without characters. Events in and of themselves cannot evoke lasting interest. If you find that hard to believe, read the obituaries or the birth announcements in an out-of-town newspaper.

What is more dramatic than birth or death? All the same, chances are you won't be able to remember any details from those columns even a day later *unless you come across the name of someone you know*.

Readers pick up books of fiction with the expectation of vicarious experience. They want to identify and become emotionally involved with the people who exist on those pages.

Your job, as author, is to create real live, three-dimensional characters for the readers. You can do this by showing how your characters look and sound, how they act and think, and why they behave the way they do.

As a mystery author, you have an added limitation: Every character who will be a serious suspect must have personality factors or motives that cause him or her to behave in a manner consistent with either guilt or innocence.

Suppose old Mr. Webster has been shot. When we show the readers that Midge is burying a revolver beneath her begonias, we want the readers to suspect her. Thus,

Midge must act and speak like a woman guilty of murder.

At the same time, we know that Midge *didn't* kill Mr. Webster. And even though the readers won't learn of her innocence until the end of the book, everything Midge says and does in the meantime must also be consistent with her innocence. Otherwise, our ending won't be believable and the readers won't feel satisfied.

This limitation—this necessity for creating characters who may either be guilty or innocent—creates a special problem for beginning mystery writers. They tend to create vague characters on the one hand or inconsistent personalities on the other.

Let's first examine the general procedures in creating a fictional character and then go on to consider the special problems that mystery stories present.

It has been said that the author must know *everything* about the characters in order to write a novel. To a beginning writer, this often seems like a lot of work—unnecessary work. What difference does it make what the hero's father did for a living if the father or his occupation are never going to be mentioned in the story?

First of all, the author must know the characters well enough to keep them consistent. For example, if you don't have a clear idea of what Arthur looks like, you might have him struggling to get into a car in Chapter 4 and vaulting a six-foot fence in Chapter 10. (Obviously, your readers won't have much of an idea what Arthur looks like, either. But it will *bother* them!)

In the same way, you need to be consistent about people's attitudes and behavior. Here's where all that background information comes in.

Suppose our hero is Lance, a successful trial lawyer. If his father was a bricklayer and Lance had to work his way through the state college and law school by taking a series of odd jobs, he'll be a very different person than if his father had been a wealthy plastic surgeon who sent his son to exclusive private schools. And we'd have yet another personality if Lance's father were a military man and the family moved from place to place all during Lance's youth.

Thus, while the father may never be mentioned in the story, the attitudes Lance has because of his father *will* be evident.

Some writers need to know their characters completely before they can even begin to plot their story. Other writers need to see their characters in action in order to understand them. They come to know their characters as the story unfolds.

There are advantages and disadvantages to either method. If you begin with well-developed characters, you may put them together and find that not much happens. It's a lot like matchmaking. Either the chemistry is there, or it isn't.

And even if your characters interact well, you may end up with an unwieldy plot. Well-developed characters have a tendency to go their own way, making it more difficult for the author to control the story.

On the other hand, if you begin writing with a well-developed plot and no clear ideas about your characters, you run the risk of failing to develop your characters thoroughly. You may end up with a story in which the people are vague or inconsistent or stereotyped. Your readers won't be able to identify with them.

Thus, whether you are better off beginning your story with a character or with a plot depends a good deal on which set of problems you are better able to handle. We'll discuss both methods here. You might like to experiment, trying to develop a story idea each way to see what happens. The more you write, the more likely you are to find that you are using a little bit of both methods.

DEVELOPING A PLOT
FROM A CHARACTER

This method of writing a story depends upon knowing your character so well that if you put him in a difficult situation, you will know what he'll do next.

How do you get to know a character this well? One way is to develop a profile. Imagine that you have an information sheet to be filled out. Let your mind run free and answer the questions with whatever occurs to you.

It is good to remember that if you select a name at this point, you may want to change it after you've gotten to know your character.

The following might be a sample profile of a major character:

CHARACTER PROFILE

VITAL STATISTICS:
  Name: (blank for now)   *Age:* 54   *Sex:* Female
  Place of birth: rural Kansas
  Present address: a small town in Kansas
  Father's occupation: Railroad ticket agent
  Mother's occupation: Housewife/Sunday school teacher
  Marital status: Widowed since age 40
  Late husband's occupation: Baker
  Children: One daughter, Alice, age 20, a student
PHYSICAL DATA:
  Height: 5'2"   *Weight:* 125   *Hair:* Short and gray
  Body type: Sturdy, plump. Short arms and legs. Round face.
  Coloring: Fair   *Eyes:* Blue   *Energy level:* High
  General health: Good   *Scars or birthmarks:* None noticeable

SOCIAL LEVEL:

Education: High school graduate. C+ student

Political persuasion: No formal affiliation—usually votes Republican

Religion: Attends Methodist church. Belongs to church-sponsored ladies' organization that raises money for needy children overseas

Other organizations: Ladies' canasta club

Hobbies: Gardening, needlepoint

At this point, let's pause and take stock. We know a lot about this woman, but she isn't very interesting. In fact, she seems downright dull. But it's important to realize that this dullness does not necessarily arise from her background. She isn't interesting to us because we don't yet know her as a living person. In order to do that, we need to know her level of awareness, her hopes and fears, her values. In a manner of speaking, we must give her a soul.

How does one do this? One way is to look behind the basic information we've collected. For example, this woman gave birth to her first and only child at the age of thirty-four. Why? Did she marry late in life? Did she have to cope with years of infertility? Was the pregnancy a happy surprise or a rude shock? Was she overprotective toward the child?

And what about the late husband? How did he die? How did she respond to his death?

Speaking of response, another way to gain insight into our character is to see how she responds to a problem. Even a small problem will often serve.

Imagine, for example, that this woman is standing in her kitchen, washing dishes. A big black ant comes running along the countertop. How will she react?

She might be alarmed at the sight of an insect in her immaculate kitchen. Perhaps, after killing it, she examines all the cupboards to make sure there aren't any more ants. Then she cleans out all her cabinets for good measure. And finally, to be on the safe side, she goes to the store and buys some ant poison.

Or she might get angry at the sight of the ant. How dare this filthy bug invade her kitchen? She squashes it, scrapes the remains into the garbage disposal, and grinds them up with satisfaction.

Or she might smile. She gently coaxes the ant onto her finger and puts it outdoors, in her garden.

Once you are sure what her response to the ant is like, you'll have a clearer picture of the woman herself. You *know* how she'll react when her twenty-year-old daughter comes home in tears and announces that she's pregnant and that her boyfriend has just left town!

And now too—after you've seen her in action—you can add further information to her profile. What are her speech patterns like? Does she speak in anxious, jerky sentences or does her voice trail off in uncertainty? Does she speak in a firm, almost dictatorial manner or in a gentle persuasive one?

How does her hair behave? Does it fall into soft, flattering (if not particularly fashionable) lines? Or is it parted sharply and cut into a severe style? Or is it perhaps fairly unmanageable?

What kind of gestures and mannerisms does she display habitually? Does she purse her lips? Bite them? Does she clench her teeth or her fists? Drum her fingers on the table? Does she smile frequently or frown a lot?

This is the point at which you ought to be thinking about a name for your character.

Choosing Names

Names serve several purposes in a story:

1. *They help the reader to keep the various characters straight.* For this reason the names you choose should be easily distinguishable. Don't put Mary, Larry, and Terry in the same

story. Or Jean, Jane, and June. Or Egbert and Albert. It's even a good idea to avoid giving two characters of similar importance the same initial.

There are, of course, exceptions, when similar names are necessary to the plot. In these cases care must be taken to avoid unnecessary confusion. In the same vein, if you have a character with an ambiguous name, such as Kelly or Leslie, be sure to establish that person's gender immediately.

2. *Names serve to characterize the people in your story.* Men with names such as Lew Archer, Travis McGee, Mike Hammer, and Sam Spade couldn't be armchair detectives any more than Hercule Poirot, Nero Wolfe, and Sherlock Holmes could be two-fisted, hard-boiled private eyes.

When you are selecting names for your characters, make sure the names are suitable to the personalities. As unfair as it may seem, certain names will conjure up particular associations in your readers' minds. A man named Wilby or Theodore, for example, will not be believable as a rowdy, illiterate sailor. On the other hand, it would be hard to accept someone named Rocky or Spike as a philosopher or an aristocrat.

Occasionally you may want to use a name that is sharply at odds with the character's personality for purposes of humor or contrast. It is usually best to do this only with minor characters.

It is also good to be aware that a married woman's last name characterizes not only her but her husband as well. Likewise a woman's maiden name can tell the readers something about her parents. Ann O'Reilly Vandergelt leaves a different impression than Ann Vandergelt O'Reilly does.

3. *Names can make your characters memorable.* Until the final draft of *Gone with the Wind*, Margaret Mitchell's heroine was named Pansy. Changing the name to Scarlett was a stroke of brilliance. Not only was it appropriate for the fiery and

tenacious woman, but it was sufficiently unusual to stick in the reader's mind long after the book was finished.

As a general rule, the more important your character, the more memorable a name he needs. Make it a habit to watch for uncommon names in newspapers and magazines. The telephone directory is another good source, as are books for naming babies. The Bible and a calendar of the saints can be useful as well.

In naming your characters, you might look for an unusual first name (Barnaby Jones) or last name (Jane Marple) or both (Asey Mayo). You can even use two common names if the *combination* is unusual. For example, take an ordinary Occidental name and an ordinary Oriental name and you have Charlie Chan. The alliteration also makes this name easy to remember.

Suppose we want to give our lady from Kansas a name. We've decided that she responded to the ant in the kitchen by grinding it up in the disposal. She's an insensitive, self-centered woman. When her daughter tells her of the pregnancy, the woman's first response is, "How could you do this to *me?*"

What kind of a name would be appropriate? Nothing dainty or overly feminine, for sure. Considering her background, she might likely have a Biblical name. A short, brusque name would be best. Ruth, perhaps.

Once you feel you know your character well, you can begin to develop the plot by giving her a problem—the bigger, the better. And remember that a mystery must deal with a crime.

In this case, since Ruth is obviously concerned with what people will think, let's set a blackmailer upon her. Suppose that Ruth's husband cheated his partner out of a great deal of money years ago and a stranger who knows this comes to town. He threatens to expose the truth unless Ruth gives him a large sum of money. Ruth is now caught. She doesn't want to be known as the widow of a common thief. What would the ladies in the canasta club say? How could she hold her head up in church?

On the other hand, the only way she can raise a large amount of money is to mortgage her home, and the bank won't give her a loan unless she tells them what she wants it for.

What will Ruth do? Here is where your story begins. If you know your character well, events will begin to unfold naturally.

HOW TO DEVELOP
A CHARACTER FROM A PLOT

Suppose you've thought of a clever way to murder someone and you want to use it in a story. Alex is going to murder Peter. Why? Because Peter has been having an affair with Alex's wife.

At this point, a beginning writer can easily be fooled into thinking that Alex's motivation is clear. But it isn't.

Alex might have chosen to divorce his wife. Or see a marriage counselor. Or go out and get drunk. Or beat up his wife. Or beat Peter up. Or have an affair himself. These are responses that others have chosen. We need to know why Alex chose murder instead.

If you can't tell the readers what makes Alex different, you'll have a plot but not a story.

Why *is* Alex driven to murder? And why does he murder Peter instead of his wife? Does he see her as a possession? Is he threatened by the thought of losing his possessions? Why? Was he deprived materially or emotionally as a child?

Or is Alex a vengeful man? Perhaps he's known Peter

for years and he's collected a series of real or imagined grievances against him. What triggered this behavior?

Ask yourself as many such questions as you can. As you answer these questions, you'll discover the emotions and conflicts that rule Alex's life.

Motivation is everything. You cannot create a vibrant character unless you know what makes him behave the way he does. In order to truly understand Alex, you have to know what happened to him. In essence, you are constructing a profile in reverse. Instead of collecting background information on a character and then deciding how that character will act in a given situation, you first decide how Alex will act and then try to figure out what kind of person he must be and how he came to be that way.

Remember, too, that you have to go through this same process with all your major characters. In this case, you'll also have to know Alex's wife and Peter thoroughly.

How do you know when you've uncovered a person's true motives?

Motives originate from fundamental needs. All human beings have certain basic needs. They have an instinct to preserve and reproduce life. They gather into communities where they promulgate rules that give order to their lives and that satisfy their perception of justice. That community may be as small as a family or as large as a nation, but each person has a need to be a part of it, to be loved and respected by himself and by the other members of the community.

Not all these needs are of equal intensity within a given person. Most people will not kill unless their lives are in danger—some not even then. The latter have a sense of order (from which springs their ideas of right and wrong) that is unusually strong. Others will kill for what seem to be trivial reasons—to impress a peer or to obtain an otherwise unimportant object. These are often people who feel power-less in their community, and they see such actions as a means to gain respect and self-esteem.

As you examine the motivations of your characters, keep asking and answering questions until you have reduced the matter at hand to a basic need. Basic needs not only produce the strongest motivations, but they also arouse greatest reader interest because everyone can identify with them to a greater or lesser extent.

Developing a Complex Character

To make a character more complex, give him conflicting motivations.

Suppose Andrew is a police detective who is investigat-ing an armed robbery and murder case. If he solves it, he stands a good chance to get the promotion he has wanted for a long time. *But* he has just uncovered some evidence that points to the son of an old friend. Furthermore, the friend has a serious heart condition and may well die if his son is charged with murder.

Now Andrew has several conflicting motivations. His sense of justice (need for order) demands turning the evi-dence in. His job as a policeman is to capture criminals and protect society. If he deliberately fails to do so, he'll suffer a loss of self-esteem as well as lose his chance at that promotion (which would give him power and added respect in the community).

On the other hand, loyalty and friendship (another sense of being part of the community) will tempt him to destroy the evidence and to protect his friend's fragile health (need to preserve life).

What will Andrew do? That will depend upon the kind of person he is—which motivations impel him most strongly.

And therein lies your story.

Motivating Villains

While you are probing your hero's motivations, it is easy to forget about the villain. But the bad guys need motives, too. And those motives have to be strong, for villains do things most people wouldn't do.

Manfred was abandoned by his parents and lived in a series of foster homes. He never felt loved until he met a beautiful Russian woman. In order to get permission to marry her from the Russian government, Manfred is giving them military secrets.

Delia was raised by a neurotic aunt who brought the girl up to be a fearful, anxious person. Desperate for a sense of security, Delia joined a religious cult that she sincerely believes is the world's last hope of survival. To help the cult carry out their work, Delia is embezzling large sums of money from the bank where she works.

These are motives that any reader can easily understand. Suppose, however, that Delia wants all that money so that she can open up a boutique. Then we'd have to ask ourselves why owning that boutique is so important to her. Is she trying to elevate herself in the eyes of her peers? Why? What happened to make her feel that she needs that recognition so badly? Was she so deprived that even a middle-class income cannot relieve her sense of insecurity? Perhaps in her mind only owning her own business will provide enough security for her to stop feeling threatened. To her owning a boutique may seem like self-preservation.

What if you are describing a person who is mentally ill? Do you have to make sense out of senseless actions? Yes, as much as possible.

Suppose you're describing Ida, an elderly woman who periodically goes walking downtown, stopping everyone with a young child. She never says a word, just peers into the child's face for a moment before moving on.

If that's all you tell your readers, they'll shrug and think, "Strange woman."

But if you let them know that fifty years ago, Ida's own young child disappeared and was never seen again, that old woman will become very real to your readers. What she's doing may not be a normal response to reality, but it *can* be understood.

It is true, too, that people may do things under certain circumstances that they would never do otherwise. A desperate situation, continuing stress, repeated provocation, drugs, and alcohol can all cause a person to lose normal inhibitions.

Nonetheless, you are not explaining motivation if you tell your readers that Monroe shot Otto because Monroe was drunk. Not everyone turns violent when intoxicated. Some get silly. Some cry. Some go to sleep. Your readers still want to know *why* Monroe pulled a gun.

To sum up, in order to truly understand a character, keep asking yourself why that character is doing what he does until you find a motivation that fulfills a basic need. Then show that motivation to your readers. As a result, your characters will become real, living people.

PUTTING THE CHARACTER ON PAPER

Once you have come to understand your characters well, how do you go about showing the readers what they are like without giving a detailed life history for each one?

Search for the dominant traits each character is going to display. In a mystery, because you are dealing with crime and the potential for committing it, you'll be particularly interested in moral weaknesses: You'll be working with people who lie, cheat, and steal. They'll be jealous and greedy and lustful.

This doesn't mean that everyone in your book is a reprobate. Your characters are simply human beings and they have faults—faults that interest us because *even small wrongdoings—the kind that everyone commits—can cast a lot of suspicion on a character if they occur at appropriate times.*

Suppose Wendell was once convicted of embezzlement, served his prison term, and has since led an honest life in a new city. When an acquaintance is murdered, however, Wendell may lie about his past out of fear that the police might try to pin the crime on him if they knew he was an ex-convict.

At a given point in the story, the readers may or may not know about Wendell's past. Either way, he can look guilty simply because he lied.

In this case you may want the readers to wonder whether Wendell lied out of evil motives (to hide the fact that he *did* commit the murder) or out of weakness (fear that he might be unjustly blamed).

At other times you may want the readers to have a pretty good idea of whether the character is evil or merely weak.

For example, suppose your plot needs a woman who is an excessively greedy person. We'll call her Bernice. There are several ways we can show the readers *what* she's like. She'll be overly concerned with her possessions—anxious to own the best of everything and at the same time determined to pay as little as possible for it. She brags about her designer dresses, yet she hesitates to lend her sister a sweater on a chilly evening. She's proud of her fine china and crystal but skimps on the food when she has dinner guests.

So far, so good. But how do we go about showing the readers *why* Bernice behaves this way?

Because we have analyzed her thoroughly, we know that she came from a very poor family and that her greed is rooted in her fear of returning to poverty. And we'll use her gestures and mannerisms to show this to the readers.

Perhaps she habitually clutches at her diamond necklace as if it were a lifeline. She shows signs of deep anxiety when a dinner guest takes a second helping of meat. She may huddle in her furs, shivering on warm days as she recounts how cold it was in the house where she grew up.

In only a few sentences we can show the readers how pathetic and afraid Bernice is. This is called delineating a character.

An Exercise in Delineating a Character

Let's say you have a character, Petra, clearly in mind. You know every last detail about her, from the violin lessons she took when she was five to the name of the perfume she wears. But you've only got a couple of paragraphs to show the readers what Petra's like. How do you do it?

You do it in the same way that an artist captures a scene with a sketch. A few lines delineate the important details and the observer is invited to fill in the rest of the picture. A writer does it with words, using a few telling details.

A telling detail is one that does the work of several. To select telling details, look at the following in your character:

1. Movements
2. Language
3. Habits
4. Ideas and attitudes
5. Values

For example, we might show that Petra (1) has an effortless, graceful walk, (2) speaks flawless English with frequent poetic turns of phrase, (3) habitually orients the bills in her wallet the same way in order of decreasing denomination, (4) believes in reincarnation, and (5) collects miniature porcelain frogs.

Given only these five facts about Petra, what else might our readers assume about her? Is her apartment usually tidy or in a mess? Is her furniture modern or French Provincial or eclectic? Will the colors in the room be coordinated? Does she own many books? What kinds? What would we find in the refrigerator? Pizza? Artichokes? Does she keep a cat? Plants? Does she have a sense of humor? Is her checking account overdrawn? How much education has she had?

Some of the answers are pretty clear. For example, if Petra is so orderly that she habitually arranges the bills in her wallet, her apartment isn't likely to be a mess. Nor is her checking account going to be overdrawn. Her flawless grammar and poetic turns of phrase indicate a liking of words; hence, she's probably pretty well educated and certainly has books around the apartment.

Some things are not clear. For example, whether or not she keeps a cat.

A good way to test whether or not you've selected the right telling details is to try them out on a few friends, almost like a parlor game. Give them a few details and ask them to tell you what this character is like. To the extent that you find general agreement on certain traits, you'll know that your details are well chosen.

Tags for Keeping Characters Straight

In a novel-length story, you'll often have several characters of lesser importance. Since you can't spend a lot of wordage describing these people, it's a good idea to select a vivid detail or "tag" for each of these characters in order to help the readers keep them straight. Some examples:

Lucy hums whenever she's trying to concentrate.

George never knows what to do with his hands and is forever fingering something.

Morgan is timid and often leaves sentences unfinished.

Gail habitually makes irrelevant remarks.

Thus, even if George hasn't been around for several chapters, when he begins to finger any little object at hand, your readers will remember him. It's as if you, the author, are saying, "You remember George, don't you? He's the fellow who . . ."

In summary, your success in putting your characters on paper depends upon two things: (1) you must first know your characters well, and (2) from all the things you know about a given character, you must learn to select the particular details that will show the readers exactly what they need to know.

5

The Protagonist
and the Villain

Special attention must be given to the creation of your protagonist—the main character in your story (and usually the one from whose viewpoint the story is told)—because the readers want to identify with him or her.

In order to aid this identification process, you must endow the protagonist with some attractive qualities. Beware, however, of overdoing it. It's tough to identify with perfection! Real people have weaknesses, and so should your protagonist. On the whole, however, good qualities should outweigh the bad ones.

This doesn't mean that your protagonist cannot be morally flawed, for the readers' admiration can be relative.

For example, suppose your protagonist is Max, a con artist who enjoys defrauding wealthy people of their cash. He draws the line, however, at preying on the helpless, the poor, or the elderly. In fact, he goes out of his way to be kind to these people.

Max has, therefore, a set of rules by which he abides, and the reader can admire him for that. As long as Max doesn't seriously harm anyone and he has some attractive qualities—say, great personal charm or a droll sense of humor—the readers will overlook the fact that he's basically dishonest.

Another instance in which the readers will identify with a flawed or unlikable protagonist is when the villain is a far worse person.

Suppose Sheila is a highly successful fashion designer who is insensitive to everyone who can't do something for her. Sheila's clawed her way to the top and has made a few enemies. One of these enemies is Alyce, a rival designer who is competing with Sheila for the coveted World Designer's Award. Alyce will stop at nothing to win. Stealing designs, blackmail, and even murder are part of her tactics.

As Sheila and Alyce vie for the award, the readers will be on Sheila's side.

The one case in which the protagonist may be completely unlikable is the biter-bit story. This is a reversal of the usual story formula. Now the protagonist is an unappealing character who is striving to achieve an evil end and the readers have every reason to believe he will succeed, although they hope he will not. In such stories, the protagonist generally brings about his own downfall, usually through one of his moral flaws. In this type of story the readers tend to remain emotionally removed from the protagonist, and interest depends more heavily upon plot.

No matter which type of protagonist you use, he or she *must take action.* There are two good reasons for this:

1. Passive characters tend to be uninteresting.
2. If your readers identify with the protagonist—that is, mentally *become* the protagonist—they will experience a kind of self-satisfaction when the protagonist solves his problem.

Hence, if Max, our con artist, is in danger of being exposed, he won't just sit tight and hope the police won't find him. He'll take active steps to confuse them.

Likewise, Sheila won't simply accept the fact that her designs are being stolen, she'll set a trap for Alyce.

The Protagonist's Physical Appearance

It is generally a good idea to make your protagonist physically appealing. Most people want to think of themselves as good-looking and resist identifying with someone who is obviously unattractive.

You can, however, have your protagonist be unaware of his or her appeal if it's suitable to your plot.

Suppose Martin is a middle-aged detective whose wife has divorced him to marry a younger man. Martin is depressed and considers himself no longer attractive to women.

When Martin investigates the murder of a wealthy industrialist, he finds considerable evidence that points to Lisa, the lovely young widow, as being the murderer. Martin's instincts, however, tell him that she is being framed, and he sets out to prove it.

At first, when Lisa is friendly toward him, Martin thinks that she is merely grateful to have someone on her side. Later, when it becomes apparent that she genuinely cares about him, Martin realizes that middle age hasn't robbed him of his manly appeal. This can make a nice subplot and add to your characterization of Martin.

That Indefinable Something

Because your protagonist is a very special person, it's often a good idea to set him or her apart from the crowd with some special characteristic. This is a particularly good idea when you are creating a series character.

Thus, Sherlock Holmes is painstakingly logical, plays

the violin, and shoots holes in his walls from time to time. Nero Wolfe is an expert on fine cuisine and rare orchids. Travis McGee lives on a houseboat. Charlie Chan spouts psuedo-Confucian sayings. Fletch has an irreverent and laser-sharp sense of humor.

Make your protagonist someone readers won't forget. Give him or her a touch of class!

Protagonists to Beware Of

1. *Dull people.* Beware of making your protagonist too ordinary. Everyone wants to think of himself or herself as being special in some way and will resist identifying with a protagonist who isn't.

2. *Bumblers.* Occasionally, stories are written in which the main character stumbles along, misinterpreting clues and misunderstanding events with comic result. Somehow, in spite of himself, he succeeds in tripping up the villain. When successful, such stories are great fun, but they are not easy to write. Reader identification—and therefore the suspense level—is fairly low and must be compensated for by a high level of humor.

The bumbling protagonist often appears in pastiches or spoofs and is easier to manage on screen—where visual gags can keep the story moving—than in a book. Inspector Clouseau and Inspector Dover are good examples of successful bumblers.

3. *Superheroes.* Readers can't feel concern for someone who is invulnerable or who has no limitations. (That's why even Superman can't see through lead and can be killed by Kryptonite.) If your protagonist wins every conflict and always anticipates and is prepared for the enemy's next move, you'll have little suspense or reader identification in your story.

4. *Bizarre types.* Beware of making your protagonist unusual to the point of being bizarre. If your heroine is Sadie, a Rumanian belly dancer with a Ph.D. in parasitology who likes to go hang gliding on weekends, you'll have very few readers stepping into her high heels.

And don't be fooled by the rationale: "But I *know* someone exactly like that!" All that proves is that you know a rather bizarre individual. It won't make it any easier for your readers to identify with Sadie. Such types are best employed as minor characters in your story.

What About Handicaps?

Chief Robert T. Ironside solved crimes from his wheelchair. And Captain Duncan Maclain and Max Carrados were blind.

Obviously a handicap is not necessarily a disadvantage for a protagonist. The key is to *have the handicap elevate the character.* He or she has become a better or stronger or wiser person in the process of learning to live with a disability.

For reasons already discussed, you don't want to have the handicap cause your protagonist to be hideously deformed or to exhibit grotesque behavior. The trick is, as always, to make your protagonist someone the reader will identify with.

The Protagonist's Occupation

The main characters in mysteries come from all walks of life. It isn't necessary to have your protagonist be a police officer or a detective. Other writers have successfully used doctors, financial experts, reporters, religious figures, lawyers, educators, and jockeys.

However, you ought not to choose your protagonist's occupation at random, for what a person does is a valuable means of characterization. An interesting job is a good way to make a character more attractive. It also gives you the opportunity to endow the character with special knowledge and abilities that he or she may use in the solution of the mystery.

It's also important to remember that unless you're writing a biter-bit story, in which your protagonist comes to a bad end, you shouldn't give him an occupation that is repulsive to your readers—for example, a drug dealer or a killer-for-hire.

There are some advantages in using an official investigator as protagonist:

1. Police have the authority to do certain things that an ordinary citizen may not do: get search warrants, subpoena records, take people into custody for questioning, run laboratory tests on evidence, and so on.

2. Police officers or professional private detectives can more easily investigate people whom they don't know personally. Furthermore, they can credibly do it at all hours and under circumstances unavailable to the lay person.

3. Police have access to scientific experts and official information that is often difficult for the ordinary citizen to obtain. Likewise, professional detectives have established networks of contacts from whom they can readily acquire information.

Douglas, an economics teacher, suspects that the button he found near Arlo's body came from a coat belonging to Sam. The police could get a warrant, seize the coat, and fairly quickly have it tested in the lab to determine whether or not the button came from it. Douglas, however, will have a much harder time linking the button to Sam.

On the other hand, there are also advantages in having your protagonist be an unofficial investigator:

1. Unofficial investigators don't have to go by the book, worry about suspect's rights during the investigation, file re-

ports, and so on. By the same token, a person unfamiliar with police procedure can accidentally ruin or overlook evidence that the police wouldn't believably miss.

2. An official investigator can easily socialize with the suspects. Thus, Douglas might attend the same dinner party as Sam. And under social circumstances, casual conversations may produce information that wouldn't logically be brought out when officials are questioning suspects.

Behavior as Related to Occupation

Whatever your protagonist's occupation, you'll need to know enough about it to make your character act believably.

Brenda is a ballerina. Obviously she won't move awkwardly across the room to meet the police investigators. But did you know that a ballerina must keep her body fat level below 15 percent of her weight? This fat level is so low that it affects the female hormonal balance, and as a consequence many professional ballerinas are infertile. How will this affect Brenda psychologically? Are there other side effects of her profession?

Is it believable to have her attend a dinner party and put away a large helping of lasagna? Would she drink a martini? How many hours a day does she have to spend dancing and exercising? Is she more likely to get cramps in her toes or her calves? What kind of street shoes does she wear?

Obviously, the best way to answer such questions is to interview a professional ballerina. If that isn't possible, you'll have to read extensively about ballet and life in it.

Occupational Language

Every profession has specialized words and phrases of its own. If Phillip is a doctor, he won't examine the body and say, "He was shot in the leg and bled to death." He'd probably say something like, "The bullet ruptured the femoral artery. He hemorrhaged to death." And your readers know this. Think of all the doctors they've seen on television!

Appropriate Physical and Mental Characteristics

Once you've chosen an occupation for your protagonist, make sure that he or she has the physical and mental abilities needed to accomplish his or her work.

For example, a historian needs a good memory for names, dates, and places. A microbiologist needs good eyesight. An artist must have a keen perception of color and physical detail.

Remember that your story will be stronger and more satisfying if your protagonist can make use of these special characteristics.

Suppose Albert is a diamond cutter. He has to have unusually steady hands and nerves. He could credibly dismantle a bomb if someone gave him the instructions over the telephone.

It is, of course, necessary for all your other characters to have occupations too, and you'll need to extend these same considerations to them to a lesser extent.

GROWTH AND DEVELOPMENT OF THE PROTAGONIST

In general, the protagonist in a novel grows and changes, as does any living human being. There is no reason why the protagonist in a mystery novel shouldn't do the same. Indeed, such growth and change—which should occur as a natural outcome of the events in your story—will enrich your book.

Suppose Paul is a police detective whose wife was accidentally killed by a housebreaker. When Conrad is later picked up for a similar housebreaking, Paul is bitterly determined to prove that Conrad is the man who killed his wife. He feels that her death will somehow be avenged if Conrad is brought to justice.

But the more Paul investigates, the less convincing the evidence becomes, and Paul ends up proving that Conrad is innocent of any crime. His desperate search for the truth, however, removes Paul's need for revenge. He realizes that setting an innocent man free is as much a tribute to his late wife as convicting a guilty man. In such a story Paul will be a wiser, more sensitive person by the end of the book. (And, we hope, so will the readers.)

Growth and Change in the Series Character

The question of growth and change creates a special problem if your protagonist is going to be a series character. Because your readers will not necessarily read your books in sequence, there must be a certain constancy about your protagonist.

One obvious solution to this problem is to create a character old enough to have a fully developed personality—that is, middle age or nearing it. A sixty-year-old may believably have much the same personality as he did at forty, but a forty-year-old who is the same as he was at twenty would be immature and unappealing.

However, if you create a mature protagonist and are fortunate enough to have your series enjoy popularity for thirty or forty years, you'll be faced with another problem: aging. What do you do when your hero gets to be a hundred and ten years old?

Different writers have solved this problem in different ways. Hercule Poirot was already retired when he first appeared in *The Mysterious Affair at Styles* in 1921. He died in the 1975 novel, *Curtain*. Dame Agatha Christie decided to have him age slowly so that, while he did grow older, he was nowhere near the age he would logically have been.

In contrast, Rex Stout solved the same problem with a straightforward approach: Nero Wolfe and Archie Goodwin never got any older! Wolfe was always in his late fifties and Goodwin in his middle thirties.

If you find it convenient not to have your protagonist undergo much change within a story, it is often a good idea to have another important character show growth or come to an important realization. Thus, the readers will still have the sense that they are watching real people who grow and change.

THE VILLAIN

It isn't always obvious to the beginning writer that as much thought and care may be required to create a villain as to create a protagonist. But the most interesting contests are those in which the adversaries are evenly matched. The readers will be most satisfied when the villain turns out to be nearly (but not *quite*) as clever as the hero.

If the villain is not to be unmasked until the end of the story, we have a special problem to contend with. On the one hand, the readers don't want to be able to guess who the villain is before the revelation. On the other hand, the readers want to be satisfied that this character is exactly the type of person who would have committed this particular crime, so that once the revelation is made, they will think, "Of course! It's obvious—why didn't we think of it?"

How can you reconcile these seemingly contradictory requirements?

The key is to remember that you can't be certain of anyone's motives unless you know what he or she is thinking. This means that while you, the author, know why everyone is behaving the way he is, the readers can only *surmise* the motives of most of your characters from what they say and do. (More about this when we discuss viewpoint in Chapter 7.)

For example, Austin refuses to leave the bedside of his wife, Rose, who is comatose following a car accident. Despite the doctors' opinions that Rose cannot understand anything he says, Austin talks to her continually, massages her muscles to counteract stiffness, and in general appears to be a devoted husband. At least, that is what one might conclude *by observation*.

Yet Austin could have underhanded reasons for staying with his wife at all times. Suppose he's afraid she *will* come to? Perhaps she was his partner in crime, and he fears that if she regains consciousness, she'll inadvertently let something slip that will incriminate him.

But if we only show Austin as a paragon of virtue, the readers won't be ready to believe us when we reveal his true nature at the end. We have to give them the feeling that the truth was there for them to see—if they had realized it. How do we do this?

The trick here is to plant certain bits of information that are consistent with Austin's guilt and/or inconsistent with his innocence and to plant such information at a time or in such a way that the readers are unlikely to see its significance.

Suppose Austin and Rose conspired to murder her brother so that she'd inherit a large sum of money. The readers, however, don't suspect this because we've presented two pieces of information that tend to obscure the couple's motives:

1. Austin and Rose are already wealthy and apparently have no desperate need for money.
2. They seem to be a very generous couple. We'll show that they allow Muriel, a penniless, feeble-minded old woman, to live rent-free in a small house on their property.

And then we'll plant one of those tricky bits of information. We'll let the readers meet Muriel and show that though she does ramble on disjointedly, she occasionally says things that make perfect sense. We won't comment on this, however; it will be up to the readers to catch it.

Now most readers won't *consciously* recognize that the woman has periods of clarity, but her behavior *will* make an *unconscious* impression.

We will let Muriel ramble on that it's only right that she pays no rent because she is the real owner of all this land. In fact, Austin and Rose ought to be paying rent to *her*. She may frown and mutter about having her lawyer check on the matter and then lapse again into obvious confusion.

If we write it carefully, 99 percent of our readers won't catch the significance of that little speech. It will be dismissed as part of the nonsense that comes of her mental deterioration. But later, when it is revealed that Austin and Rose actually *did* defraud Muriel of her land, that unconscious impression that Muriel isn't completely batty will surface. The readers will think, "Of course! We really knew that! Why didn't we believe her when she said it was actually her land?"

And, of course, once they accept Austin and Rose as capable of defrauding a feeble-minded woman, it's not difficult to believe they would commit murder out of greed.

There is one other thing that must be said about the creation of a villain. Imagine that you pick up your morning paper and read that three men have each robbed a different bank. The first man is a complete stranger. The second is a vague acquaintance. The third bank robber is your next-door neighbor, a fellow you've known for years. Which of the three stories will capture your attention?

The readers are most interested—and therefore most satisfied—when the villain turns out to be a familiar character. Accordingly, the villain should appear early and often in your story and should be as important a character as possible.

6
Settings

The setting for a story is an integral part of it. No matter how fundamental the story line is, *where* it happens will make a difference.

Suppose Tom has been seeing Ed's daughter, Marlene. Ed disapproves, and the two men have a bitter argument. Now if the argument takes place in a crowded restaurant, the men are likely to control themselves for a longer period of time. Their voices, at least initially, will be lower than if they were elsewhere.

On the other hand, if they are going at it in a boiler room of a factory, they are likely to be shouting from the onset, just to be heard over the noise. They'll be dressed differently. They'll be uncomfortably warm. Tempers will be shorter. The potential for violence is greater.

And if the argument in the restaurant ends in murder, there will be witnesses. The killer will have to try to run and hide. But if the murder takes place in the boiler room, he could possibly hide the body and try to resume a normal life.

Besides actually affecting the plot, a setting can do a number of things in your story:

1. It can help to delineate a character.
2. It can provide information necessary to the plot.
3. It can make otherwise implausible behavior seem plausible.

4. It can help to foreshadow future events and to avoid the appearance of contrivance.
5. It can help to keep the reader in the fantasy.
6. It can be used to indicate the state of mind of the protagonist.
7. It can help to enhance the atmosphere of your story.

Let us consider these points in turn.

PURPOSES SERVED BY
THE CHOICE OF SETTING

The setting can be used to help delineate a character. For example, look what the setting in the following passage does:

> Dorian turned the key and slipped into Dr. Hudson's office. The room was enormous. The left wall was lined with a bank of filing cabinets and a long table upon which were several neat stacks of papers and periodicals.
>
> He crossed the room to the large oak desk. The drawers were all locked. Beside the telephone was a silver-framed photograph of a familiar-looking young woman. Dorian's heart skipped a beat as he read the inscription: "To Father, with love, Helen."
>
> He frowned. Why had she changed her name? Or had Dr. Hudson changed his?
>
> His attention turned to the shelves full of books along the right wall. *Subliminal Persuasion, Techniques of Mind Control, Hypnotic Induction, Brainwashing: Fact or Fiction?* All the titles ran along similar lines.
>
> The filing cabinets, like the desk drawers, were all locked securely. Dorian found the file drawer marked "Cases Discontinued" and went to work on the lock. He opened it in less than a minute.
>
> There were only three manila folders in the drawer. One was marked Jolene Marwell. Quickly he photo-

graphed the documents inside. Then he replaced the folder and locked the cabinet. Except for a tiny scratch on the lock, no one would know he'd been there.

As he was leaving, Dorian saw a neatly lettered sign beside the door.

Power goes to him who seizes opportunity.

"Right on, Dr. Hudson," Dorian murmured.

Even if we have not yet met Dr. Hudson, we know a great deal about him from having seen his office. The number of filing cabinets and neatly stacked papers indicate a high degree of organization. The large desk, the book titles, and the motto beside the door show us that Dr. Hudson is very concerned with personal power over others and is probably ruthless when it comes to acquiring that power. All those locked drawers in the locked office suggest that he is a man of many secrets.

By giving a bit of thought to the setting in which a character operates, whether it is where he or she works, lives, or plays, we can show our readers a great deal about that character.

The setting can provide information necessary to the plot. Remember that photograph Dorian saw on Dr. Hudson's desk? That photograph told him that Helen was Dr. Hudson's daughter, a fact he hadn't known. If, for purposes of the plot, no one can tell Dorian Helen's true identity, then the photograph is a natural and efficient way to give him this information.

If you stop to think about it, a lot of small bits of information can be gathered from one's surroundings:

A lighter, rectangle-shaped area on a wall can indicate that a mirror or a picture once hung there.

A well-defined dust-free spot on a mantle can show that a candlestick was recently moved.

Indentations in a carpet may show how the furniture was previously arranged.

Discoloration in a small area of a lawn may show that it has recently been dug up and replaced.

Sometimes, by arranging our setting properly, we can derive very specific information from it. Suppose the area around the old Hanson mill is the only place in the county where red clay is found. If Luthor goes out for a walk and returns with red clay on his shoes, we have a way of knowing where he has been even if he is not willing to say.

It is important to remember, however, that if we construct a setting so that it will convey certain information, it ought not to be a setting that is geologically impossible. Our readers will have no patience with us if we insist on putting a marsh on a mountainside just so that our plot will work out.

Proper setting can make otherwise implausible behavior seem plausible. For example, suppose a stranger approached you on the subway and offered you a chocolate. Would you accept it?

Now suppose you're at an elaborate dinner party where there are a large number of guests. Your hostess has had to employ a catering service for the evening. A young man dressed in a waiter's uniform offers you a chocolate from a silver tray.

Will you hesitate to accept it because you have never seen the man before? Will it even occur to you that the sweet may be laced with strychnine?

Similarly, in a particular setting, a fictional character may believably do things that would otherwise be implausible:

A young mother may hand her baby to a stranger at the scene of a serious accident.

A conservative, middle-aged banker who ordinarily does nothing more strenuous than open the *Wall Street Jour-*

nal may turn into an enterprising pioneer if he is stranded in the wilderness.

An introverted young man might behave in a very extroverted manner if he found himself at a costume party where no one knew him—particularly if everyone was wearing masks.

A loud-mouthed, bad-tempered woman might be surprisingly meek in church or in the dentist's chair.

Proper use of setting can foreshadow future events and help to avoid the appearance of contrivance in the plot. In Chapter 1 we said that one of the things readers like in a mystery is a sense of unity. A good way to provide it is by using the technique of foreshadowing events.

Suppose we are going to have Irene try to push young Rupert off a cliff at the climax of our story. Certainly our readers must be aware of the existence of the cliff before Irene lures Rupert to the edge of it. Thus, the first time the readers are brought into the area, the cliff should be pointed out. The height and the steepness of its walls should be clearly shown. The readers must be aware of possible peril.

It would be especially satisfying if we could open our story with a view of the cliffs and if it were mentioned at various points in the book. Then when the climax occurs, it will seem to have occurred naturally. Our readers will reason that if *they* have been aware of the cliff and how dangerous it is, it was only to be expected that Irene should think of it when she's looking for a way to kill young Rupert.

Also, by making the readers aware of the cliff from the very beginning, we'll provide that satisfying feeling at the climax of having come full circle and arriving back where we started.

Using the setting properly can also help to avoid the appearance of contrivance. Suppose Roger and Nathan are quarreling in Roger's study:

"Get off my property!" Roger shouted. "I don't ever want to see you here again!"

"It isn't exactly your property," Nathan said evenly. "It's Felice's, too. And she *did* invite me."

"Until she comes of age, it's *mine!*" Roger reached for a pistol from the antique gun collection on the wall and pointed it at Nathan. "It's loaded. Now, get out of here, or I'll use it!"

Now, suppose at this point our readers are frowning and thinking, "Wait a minute! We didn't know there was an antique gun collection on that wall!" It seems to them that we've pulled the collection out of thin air—that is, we've contrived this part of our story. Worse, we've put our readers in the uncomfortable position of having to go back and revisualize Roger's study. In the process, we've jolted them out of our fictional world.

In order to avoid doing this, we should have mentioned the gun collection the first time we showed our readers the study. The bigger the part the guns play in the plot, the more attention we must draw to them. Then when Roger takes the gun from the wall, it will seem entirely natural.

It is also important to consider the opposite situation: Suppose we imagine Roger to be the type of man who collects antique guns, but the fact that he collects them and the guns themselves will play no part in the plot.

Now, if in describing the study, we call a great deal of attention to the guns, our readers will expect them to be important. If they are not used, the readers will be disappointed. Thus, if we are going to mention them at all, it should only be in passing, as a comment on the decor of the room.

The setting can be used to help keep readers firmly in the fictional reality we have created. Try to recall the happiest experience you ever had. Or the most frightening. What exactly do you remember? Usually, barring traumatic repression, we remember a lot of little details associated with strong feelings. And most often, they are sensory details.

Suppose Frank and Greta fall in love. The affair is brief but passionate. Many years later, he'll still remember the scent of the perfume she wore, the color of the polish on her nails, the silkiness of her hair. She'll remember the song that was playing when they kissed for the first time, the taste of the wine, the way his eyes lighted up as she entered the room.

We all have memories that evoke sensory details. *And conversely, the sensory details evoke the memories.* Today, if Frank catches a whiff of the perfume Greta used to wear, he thinks of her.

On the other hand, try to remember the song that was playing in the elevator in the department store you were in last week. How about the color of the blouse the supermarket cashier was wearing the day before yesterday?

What's the difference? Why do we remember some things in great detail and others hardly at all?

The key is *emotion.* Any experience in which our emotions are raised to a high pitch will impress deeply upon our memories those sensory details that we perceived at the time.

When we write a mystery or suspense story, we are trying to generate a great deal of emotion in our readers. For the most part, we are trying to generate anxiety, but sometimes we want our readers to feel sad, happy, compassionate, or angry. In order to make the emotional experience seem real, we have to provide the readers with the same sort of sensory detail they would be aware of if they were actually living the fictional experience.

Thus, as a writer, you need to develop the habit of noticing details. What do you see? How can you describe it so the readers will see it? How *does* that new cold medicine taste? What do you smell when you step out of your front door? When you walk into the dentist's office? How would you describe the funny noise your car made just before it stopped running?

By providing appropriate sensory details, you can make your readers feel that they are truly in your protagonist's shoes, experiencing exactly what he or she is going through.

Your setting can also help to create the illusion of reality by providing a background that establishes your characters as living human beings who must experience the same daily events that your readers do. Thus, your characters must take time to eat and sleep, wash and dress, to commute to work and pick up the groceries.

This principle is especially useful when you have sections which are primarily concerned with the thoughts of the protagonist. If, for example, Sam is trying to figure out whether or not Heidi could have known about Uncle Bennet changing his will, you might have to present a couple of pages of Sam's thought processes. In the meantime, your readers have no clear mental images before them. You are presenting them simply with a sequence of ideas.

But if, while he is thinking, Sam is also shaving and dressing and gulping down a cup of coffee, he will seem a little more like a real human being, and your readers will not feel that the action in your story has come to a complete halt.

By the same principle, it is often useful to have long conversations take place over dinner. Then your readers can mentally watch your characters dining as they talk.

Time is another element that is always a part of the background of your story. It, too, helps in creating the illusion of reality. Human beings have a very real need to orient themselves in time as well as in space. To illustrate, imagine a man suddenly waking from a coma. The first two questions he'll ask are almost certain to be "Where am I?" and "What time is it?" (Or, "What day is it?")

Readers have a similar need to orient themselves in time. Your fictional world will seem more real if your readers

know what time of year it is, what day of the week, and what
time of day.

On the other hand, unless you specify to the contrary,
your readers will assume that your story is taking place in the
present year. If you take care not to unnecessarily date your
story, it can remain a good present-day story for a number of
years.

As a rule, it's a good idea to be vague about things that
change a lot, such as hemlines and the widths of lapels, ties
and hat brims. If you say, "Margie wore an unfashionably
short skirt," your readers will imagine a skirt that is notice-
ably shorter than whatever is in style at the time. As the years
pass and hemlines go up and down, the effect of that sentence will stay pretty much the same.

If, however, you say, "Margie wore a skirt that stopped
three inches above her knees," you'll be saying one thing
about Margie if your story is read in a year when hemlines
are above the knees and another if it is read when hemlines
are below them.

Depending on when the story is read, Margie may seem
like a young woman who is in the forefront of high fashion
or someone who is several years behind. She may come
across as a suitably dressed young woman or somewhat of an
exhibitionist.

By the same reasoning, avoid describing current fads or
newsworthy events as part of your background. Avoid saying
in what year the action is taking place unless it could take
place at no other time.

Time has another great importance in your story, for its
passage places certain limits on what happens. Your characters must always obey the rules of the physical universe. So if
Allen drives from San Francisco to Santa Barbara, he can't
make the trip in half an hour. He can't interview fifty people
in the same day. And even if he's an athlete of Olympic

caliber, your readers won't believe that he can swim across a river in the morning, run after a thief for three miles before lunch, chase a mysterious figure up twenty flights of stairs in the afternoon, and survive three fist fights before bedtime.

It is often helpful to make a timetable of events in your story. That way, you can make sure that what happens is not only physically possible but believable as well.

The setting can be used to indicate the state of mind of the protagonist. What you notice at a given time and place and how you perceive it depends upon your state of mind. Since a great deal of fiction is written as if events were being seen through a character's eyes, what details we choose to present to the readers and the way we choose to present them will depend upon what is going on in the mind of the protagonist.

If Harriet is late for work, she isn't likely to notice that her neighbor's crocuses are up. Nor will she hear the birds singing as she runs to the bus stop.

She probably *will* notice the bus driver. Since she usually takes an earlier bus, she will be unfamiliar with this driver and will wonder whether he usually keeps to the schedule or tends to run late.

Because she has been running and she's feeling anxious, she'll notice that the air in the bus is stuffy. Of all the passengers, she'll focus on the man who's glowering, the woman who's fretting, the child who's whining. Her attention is drawn to them because they are reflecting her own feelings. She's angry with herself for being late, anxious about the possible consequences, and irritable because of the pressure she's under.

Everything Harriet notices should be consistent with her state of mind. What happens if you select inappropriate details in describing the setting? Let's see.

Ross panted as he ran down Harrison Avenue. He had less than thirteen minutes to find Zeke and get him on the phone to Los Angeles. If he failed, Dulcie's life was as good as over.

He bumped into an old woman, sending her packages flying. "Sorry," he gasped as he ran on, knowing she couldn't have heard him.

Brakes screeched as Ross crossed Wellfleet Street. He must have run out against the light. Not that it mattered. Nothing mattered except getting to Zeke in time.

He caught sight of the big clock in front of the First National Bank. Nine minutes left and he still had three blocks and two flights of stairs to go.

Please, Zeke, be in your office! As he came to the corner of Harrison and Baker, he noticed that the mailbox on the corner had been given a fresh coat of paint. It gleamed red and blue in the sun.

He leaped over an aging cocker spaniel in front of the deli. Less than six minutes now.

How did you feel when you came to the freshly painted mailbox? Certainly there *are* mailboxes on street corners and they *do* get painted from time to time. Yet, Ross's noticing this particular detail seems incongruous. Why?

Let's look at the other things he is aware of—the things that seem right. The old woman. As a matter of fact, he doesn't notice her until he bumps into her. The brakes screeching. Again, he isn't even aware of the car until it nearly hits him. The clock. He notices this because time is of crucial importance. The names of the streets. Again, it is important to know how much farther he has to go. The cocker spaniel. He notices it only because it is in his way—an obstacle which stands between him and his goal.

Obviously, there are lots of other details in this setting that Ross isn't aware of at this time. Car horns honking. Other pedestrians. Lampposts and fire hydrants. There may even be a fat man in purple pants operating a jackhammer on the sidewalk, but Ross won't notice him unless he runs into the man or trips over the electrical cable to the jackhammer. *What we notice depends upon our state of mind.*

Similarly, our state of mind colors the way we perceive things. Suppose Stanley is on a moonlit beach in the Caribbean, waiting for Carmen, the woman he loves. Although it is a warm, humid night, Stanley is not at all uncomfortable. The gentle slapping of the waves upon the sand is soothing. A launch goes by and he watches the reflection of the running lights dance on the water.

When an occasional breeze arises, Stanley enjoys the feel of the soft air against his face and is aware of the scent of tropical flowers mingling with the salty air. He glances at the villa to his left, where Carmen lives with her parents. It is beautiful; fresh white stucco gleaming in the moonlight, intricate grillwork around the windows, lush banks of poinsetta bushes lining the walk.

The windows on this side of the villa have been dark, but now a light flashes on above the front entrance. Stanley's heart leaps. Carmen is coming!

Now let's have Stanley see the same setting, but under very different circumstances:

Stanley is again on the beach, but this time he is waiting for Carmen's body to wash ashore. He is familiar with the currents in the area as well as the tides and he has calculated that the body should wash up before dawn. He must remove a bracelet from her wrist—a bracelet he gave her and which can be traced back to him.

Although the temperature is no higher than before, it now seems uncomfortably hot to Stanley. He is sweating profusely. When the breeze rises, he stiffens. Is he hearing only the rustle of the palms, or is someone coming?

The launch goes by, its motor and running lights striking terror in Stanley's heart. Will anyone aboard spot Carmen's white skirt billowing on the water?

Stanley is aware of the smell of fear coming from his own body and mingling with the odor of some half-rotted seaweed that has been washed up. The steady slapping of the waves is getting on his nerves.

To his left, the villa stands dark and ominous in the moonlight. Suddenly, a light flashes on above the front door. Stanley is terrified. Someone's coming!

As we can see, the very same tropical beach evokes difference responses from Stanley. When he is in love, everything is beautiful. When he is afraid, everything seems threatening. *How we see things depends upon how we feel.*

The setting can help to enhance the atmosphere of your story. What's the difference between setting and atmosphere? When we talk about settings, we are talking about the material objects in a particular place and the bodily sensations they provide—the sights and sounds, the tastes and odors and physical feelings. When we talk about atmosphere, we are talking about a frame of mind or a mood.

To understand this difference a little better, let's imagine an old, deserted mansion at the far end of town. Darkness is falling and the wind has picked up, making a loose shutter somewhere bang repeatedly. Inside, the paint on the walls is peeling and the floor boards creak. Cobwebs and dust are everywhere. The wind howls down the chimney. Through the cracked windowpane, we see a bolt of lightning rip across the sky, followed a moment later by a crash of thunder.

There is our setting. You might think that it pretty much establishes the atmosphere as well, but wait!

Here are two station wagons pulling up in front of the house. The doors of the cars fly open and fifteen eleven-year-old girls scramble out, giggling and squealing. Courtney Ash is going to have a birthday party in a "haunted house." One station wagon pulls away and the driver of the other,

Miss Faversham (a good friend of Courtney's mother) helps the girls drag their sleeping bags into the mansion before it starts to rain. Miss Faversham's great-uncle owns the mansion and she has a certain fondness for the old place. When Courtney suggested a party there, Miss Faversham thought it was a wonderful idea and volunteered to chaperone.

The girls set themselves up in the parlor and soon things are underway. One of the girls has a battery-operated cassette player and by candlelight they enjoy pizza, Pepsi, and birthday cake along with the latest hit songs. The music and laughter nearly drown out the sound of the rain lashing at the windows.

Then Courtney insists that everyone sit in a circle around a single candle. They are going to tell ghost stories. Each tale is more preposterous than the one before. Miss Faversham smiles as the old house is filled with shrieks of mock horror and nervous giggles.

Now we have an atmosphere. We know the frame of mind our characters are in. They are enjoying themselves immensely. And our setting enhances this atmosphere, for it wouldn't be nearly as much fun to spend the night telling ghost stories in the living room of the neat suburban house where Courtney lives.

And just as we can change settings without changing the atmosphere, we can change the atmosphere without changing settings.

Suppose Miss Faversham is induced to tell a story and she relates how, many years ago, a young servant girl mysteriously disappeared from this very house. Suddenly there is a bloodcurdling scream from an upstairs room. A draft rushes through the parlor and blows the single candle out.

For a moment the girls are too stunned to say anything. Then a bolt of lightning cracks through the air outside, striking a nearby tree. Fifteen screaming girls huddle around Miss Faversham, who wonders what she should do.

The atmosphere of fun has been dissolved and replaced with one of uncertainty and fear. Interestingly enough, however, our setting is now enhancing *this* mood. A scream in the night would be far less frightening in the comfortable familiarity of Courtney's well-lighted living room. Nor would the situation be so frightening if there were friendly neighbors nearby.

Another point should be made here. Don't forget the part that weather plays in creating an atmosphere. It is an effective way to enhance the mood we are trying to get our readers into.

At Courtney's birthday party, we put a thunderstorm in the background. What did this accomplish? First of all, everyone has some fear of lightning, even if they call it "healthy respect." Lightning, is after all, dangerous. And loud noises, such as thunderbolts, are unsettling.

When Courtney's party is in full swing and spirits are high, the lightning storm adds tension and heightens the excitement. (Remember that we're keeping the storm in the background here, nearly drowning it out with music and laughter.)

Then, when the scream is heard and the candle goes out, the girls fall silent. The bolt of lightning striking nearby brings the storm into immediate focus. And now it adds to the sense of vulnerability and isolation our characters experience. It's a lot harder to go running out of a house into a thunderstorm than into a clear summer night.

As a general rule, it's a good idea to ask yourself what kind of mood you want your readers to be in during a particular scene. Then ask yourself what kind of weather would contribute to that mood.

Obviously we have some limitations: We can't have a heat wave one day and a blizzard the next. Nor can we have a thunderstorm at four o'clock if the sky was cloudless at two. Weather is a steady progression of events and we must lay groundwork for anything we want to have happen.

What if your protagonist is going through a series of ups and downs during a single day? You'll have to decide which scene during that day is the most important. Then figure out what kind of weather conditions would enhance the atmosphere of that scene. Let those conditions build up gradually, the way they do in real life.

It's easy to overlook weather as part of the background of your story, but unless you are writing about events that take place underground or in windowless buildings, it should be there.

MAKING THE SETTING
A NATURAL PART OF THE STORY

A mystery or suspense story cannot afford to have periods when reader interest flags. It is important that our readers feel that something is happening at all times. Long sections of narrative, especially descriptive narrative, tempt readers to skip over them.

How, then, do you describe your setting in vivid detail without interrupting the flow of the story? Here are a few tricks.

Inject descriptive details into the story at a time when the protagonist would naturally be aware of them. If your character is in his kitchen having breakfast, that is the time to put in details about his kitchen. It is not the time to discuss the outside of the house or the neighborhood he lives in *unless he is thinking about those things for a particular reason.*

For example, he might be drinking his coffee and wondering whether he ought to have the outside of the house painted before he puts it up for sale. Or perhaps he ought just to have the peeling window trim redone. He might think that he'll be happy to move away from this neighborhood because of the rising crime rate.

On the other hand, if he's preoccupied with the problems at the office while he's buttering his toast, we should save the description of the exterior of the house and the conditions in the neighborhood until we show him coming out of the house and driving through the neighborhood. At that time, those details will be a natural part of the scene and our readers will not feel that we have interrupted the story to give them this information.

Inject descriptive details into the story little by little. When you walk into a room for the first time, you are not aware of every detail in the room at once. You become aware of the things around you gradually, particularly if you are busy talking, thinking, or doing something. Thus, you need not feel that as soon as your character enters a new scene, you have to stop everything and fully describe the setting before anything can happen. In fact, that would interrupt the flow of the story.

What you want to do is give the readers a detail here and there *in the order in which the protagonist would naturally be aware of them.* Thus, any unusual things in the room must be mentioned immediately. It would be difficult to convince your readers that your protagonist was in a room for five minutes before he noticed the full-size stuffed polar bear by the window.

On the other hand, he might easily fail to notice the clock on the wall until he finds that his watch has stopped and he looks around for a clock.

As much as possible, inject background details into the action of the story. If you want your readers to know that Jacob has a large mahogany armoire that stands beside the window in his room, don't *tell* the readers:

> The large mahogany armoire stood by the window in Jacob's room.

Instead, *show* them:

> Jacob removed a gray tweed jacket from the large
> mahogany armoire that stood by his window. As he but-
> toned the jacket, he reflected that it was time he changed
> his will again.

Now your readers are aware of the armoire, but aware
of it as part of the background to the action of the story.

With a little practice, you can learn to do this—to integrate the description of the background into the story in such
a way that the action continues even as the setting is being
described. You can still color your story with vivid details
without tempting your readers to skip sections of narrative.

UNFAMILIAR SETTINGS

Obviously the easiest place to set a story is one with which you
are entirely familiar. You know the physical lay of the land,
the flora and the fauna. You know what kind of people live
there, how they think and feel, what they do and how they
talk. You're familiar with all the little sensory details you
need to fill in your scenes.

But some stories demand to be set in other places—
some place you may have been to long ago and have half-
forgotten, or even a place you're never seen.

What do you do then?

An Unfamiliar Setting
in Your Own Country

Let's start with the easiest situation: an unfamiliar place in
your own country. You need to know something about the
geography and how it affects the people who live there. You

can't write a story set in San Francisco without being aware that the city is a port and is built on hills. The hills will make a difference in how long it takes to walk from one place to another and in how you park your car. They'll affect how far you can see and what you can see from a given spot. Assuming there's no fog, of course.

You ought to know the major landmarks. The names of important streets and where they are in relation to one another. You should know which trees are indigenous to the region, and perhaps a few flowers and birds as well.

Homes are a reflection of the people who live in them and should not be ignored. Be familiar with various styles of architecture and where they are commonly found. An average home in Vermont will look very different from an average home in New Mexico.

Homes are also a reflection of the geology and the climate of the area. If there are quarries nearby, you are likely to see a lot of homes with stone facings. Stucco is popular in the warmer parts of the country, but a stucco house will crack in the cold weather of the far north, so they are rarely found in that region. Where winters are mild, jalousie windows are popular. And in areas that experience high winds, roofs are constructed with planks instead of plywood.

And the climate itself is important. If your character is going for a walk on the beach in New Jersey on an April morning, will a sweater be warm enough? What if he's going out on a February night in Austin, Texas?

Local specialized weather effects can be a good touch for your story. The hot dry Santa Ana winds of southern California bring on dust storms and brush fires and, some say, temporary insanity in certain people. The chinook winds in the Rockies cause daily temperatures to fluctuate so wildly that there are documented cases of window glass shattering from the rapid temperature changes. It is not unusual for a chinook to cause several inches of snow to *evaporate* (not melt!) in a single day.

And what will your characters wear as they go about life in this setting? While there is a certain homogeneity in the way Americans dress in general, there are regional differences. Local people can always spot a tourist.

Then, too, if your characters are going to eat during your story, you should be aware that local customs in dining and the names of some foods vary in different regions of the country. Will your Oregon diner advertise pancakes, hotcakes, griddlecakes, or flapjacks? A Wisconsinite who orders regular coffee expects coffee that is not decaffeinated. A Massachusetts resident will expect coffee with milk in it.

What do the people do for a living in this area? That will make a big difference in what is important to them. The inhabitants of a small fishing village in Maine will be concerned with weather and tides and the size of the catches brought in recently. People in Detroit will worry about the prices of steel and oil and how they will affect the sale of cars. Natives of Montana will talk about the market price of beef and whether or not the water table is too low this year.

Unless you select a small ethnic area in the United States, you can assume that your characters will speak standard English and need only to bone up on a few colorful phrases to depict the local idioms. In general, except for an occasional word or two, it is best not to try to imitate accents or dialects in a mystery story. It is enough to remind the reader now and then that the man from South Carolina drawls and the lady from Boston speaks in a proper, clipped manner. The reader will do the rest of the work, imagining how these people sound.

If you feel compelled to throw in a few words to actually show the readers how your characters pronounce them, beware! You may think you're doing your readers a service by telling them that Roscoe said, "Ah'd lak some beckon 'n aigs, if'n y'all don' min', m'am," but that sentence is going to stop a lot of readers in their tracks. It will take them a moment or two to figure out what Roscoe meant, and in the meantime, they'll have been jolted out of your fictional world.

Foreign Settings

If you are going to tell a story that takes place in another country, you must know all the things you needed to know for an unfamiliar setting in this country—the lay of the land, the flora and fauna, the weather and climate, the architecture, the styles of dress, the common foods, and what people do for a living.

On top of that, you should know something about the country's history and current political situation and how it affects the outlook of the people you are writing about.

Even if your main characters are all American—say, they're attending a scientific conference in Spain or making a movie in Yugoslavia—it may be important to know how the local people react to them. Do they like Americans and try to imitate their ways? Or do they look upon them with contempt? Or are they suspicious of the Americans?

You will have to do some research into daily life. If your protagonist is an American staying at a hotel, can he drink the water? Can he take a shower? Does he have to do anything special to get hot water? How does she find an English language newspaper? What kind of transportation will she use to get from one place to another? What are the names of the common coins and currency?

Then, too, you must know something about the local customs. If your protagonist is in Saudi Arabia, he had better not show the soles of his shoes while he's sitting. Nor should he ever offer anyone his left hand. Both actions are regarded as extremely rude.

The Use of Foreign Languages

You can give your foreign-setting story a nice bit of color by using a little of the local language. But don't forget that the main objective is still to tell a story. That means that your readers must be able to understand what you are saying. And they should be able to understand it without any momentary confusion that jolts them out of your fantasy.

How do you use foreign language without running the risk of losing or confusing the readers? One thing you can do with little danger is to inject phrases that are so well known that most readers will understand them. For example, almost anyone knows the meaning of *Buenos dias, Merci,* or *Ach, Himmel!*

Another thing you can do is to use a word or phrase that is so similar to the English equivalent that the readers will understand immediately what it means.

"*Pardon, monsieur*, your table is waiting."

"*El teléfono, señor.* You may take it in the library."

"*Herr Stein ist ein konservativ.*"

Notice that it does not bother the readers if one sentence is in the foreign language and the next is in English. It's even all right to put only a phrase into the foreign language and leave the rest in English. But don't jump back and forth between the two. Look what happens:

"*Bonjour, madame.* Sit down, *s'il vous plaît.*

Would you like some *café au lait?*"

All the foreign words are easily understandable, but the effect of that speech is still confusing.

Yet another way to inject a foreign word or phrase effectively is to put it into a context that makes the meaning clear.

The utensils had all been removed from the table and I
had nothing with which to stir my coffee. I caught the
eye of a nearby waiter.

"Una cuchara, por favor."

A problem that arises occasionally when dealing with
foreign languages is that you may need to indicate that a
person is speaking in another language, but what is being
said is not likely to be understood by the reader if it is not in
English.

Suppose Sebastian and Roberto are in a tavern and
Sebastian invites Roberto to come with him and some of his
friends. Maria, the barmaid, hears this. We know that Maria
and Roberto speak Spanish and that Sebastian does not. We
want Maria and Roberto to have a short conversation in
Spanish. The readers must know what is being said and at
the same time must realize that Sebastian does not understand.

How do we handle this? If we put the whole conversation into Spanish, the readers won't understand it. If we put
it into English, they may wonder why Sebastian doesn't react
to what is being said. How can we solve the problem?

Maria began to clear the table. *"No te vayas con ellos,"* she
said softly. "Don't go with them. They plan to kill you."

"Esta bien." He smiled at her. "It's all right. I am prepared."

"Okay, you two! That's enough sweet talk!" Sebastian
grinned at Roberto. "Let's get going."

By beginning the speech in Spanish and immediately
translating what we have said, we have made it clear to the
readers that the conversation is being carried on in Spanish,
even though the rest of it will be given to the readers in
English. We've even played it extra safe by showing from
Sebastian's remarks that he doesn't realize what Maria and
Roberto have just said.

Historical Settings

Remember what we said earlier about readers having a strong need to orient themselves in time? When you do a story with a historical setting, you need to expend extra effort to help your readers imagine that they are in a different era.

The principle is simple: Your readers will tend to conjure up images with which they are most familiar. If you are telling a story that takes place in 1837 and you write, "Elizabeth lit the lamp in the parlor," some readers will think of a kerosene lamp because that's the oldest kind of lamp they are familiar with.

But if you say, "Elizabeth took the jar of whale oil and filled the lamp," they'll think, "That's right. They *did* use whale oil in lamps back then." Or perhaps, "I didn't know they used *whale oil* in lamps!"

Either way, the overall effect is a satisfying one. In the first case the readers feel the rightness of the detail. In the second there is the pleasant surprise of learning something new.

But, on the other hand, if you inject an inappropriate detail, for example, mentioning the state of Texas, you are sure to have a certain number of readers who know that Texas didn't become a state until 1845. And once your readers catch you falsifying one detail, they'll be reluctant to accept your word on the others. It's harder for them to suspend their disbelief and imagine that they really are in another time period.

As with other unfamiliar settings, you'll need to research clothing and furniture, architecture, the customs of the day, quirks of the language, popular foods, economic constraints, and historical events that were taking place at that time.

If you're working with a particular location—say, Jackson Hole, Wyoming in 1900—you'll need to know what it looked like at that time, the names of some of the families who lived there (but make sure that your criminals and otherwise undesirable characters have ficticious names and do not significantly resemble any of the real settlers of that time), what the occupations of the local people were, and so forth. The more detail that fits naturally into your story, the better.

How do you decide how much research is enough? In general, this is a judgment call. You need to be sure that what you do describe is accurate and that you are not omitting anything that obviously ought to be there.

If you set a story in mid April of 1865 and none of your characters seem to be aware of Lincoln's assassination, your readers are sure to find your story unrealistic.

How do you go about digging out all the details you need? We'll discuss that in Chapter 8, when we talk about research.

7
Point of View

Selecting the proper point of view from which to tell your story is a critical decision. You are, in effect, deciding what information your readers will and will not have, what emotions they will experience, with which characters they will sympathize, and what feelings they will have at the end of the story.

Consider the following plot idea: Arthur murders his wife, Millicent, and makes it look like an accident. Sarah, Arthur's stepdaughter, suspects the truth. Dan, an insurance investigator, is trying to establish what actually happened.

Because readers tend to identify with that person from whose point of view the story is told, the selection of the point of view is also a decision about the kind of story we are going to tell.

Suppose we decide to tell this story from Dan's point of view. The readers will step into his shoes. They'll know nothing about the relationships among Arthur, Sarah, and Millicent except what Dan is able to learn in the course of his investigation.

His goal—to determine exactly how Millicent died—is now theirs. Their energies will be directed toward trying to figure out what happened, who did it, and how to prove it. They will feel satisfaction when Dan captures Arthur.

We could also tell the story from Sarah's point of view.

Now the readers will step into the shoes of a young woman whose mother has died suddenly under questionable circumstances. Because the readers are in Sarah's mind, they know how Sarah got along with her mother and stepfather. They also know as much as Sarah knows about the relationship between Arthur and Millicent.

Sarah's life may be in danger if Arthur realizes that she suspects him. And now along comes Dan, a young insurance investigator who is ready to write off Millicent's death as accidental. Can Sarah convince him otherwise? Can he help her prove that her stepfather is a murderer? How will Sarah protect herself?

Sarah's goals are a little different from Dan's. Now the readers are not so much concerned with who did it or why but with how it was done and how to prove it. And how to maintain Sarah's safety in the meanwhile. They'll feel satisfaction when Arthur is caught. They'll also feel relief that Sarah is out of danger.

We could even tell the story from Arthur's point of view. We might see that Millicent was a horrible tyrant who took sadistic pleasure in making poor Arthur miserable. She manipulated him and bullied him until he felt he had no choice but to kill her. Although the murder was committed on impulse, the terrified Arthur tried to make it look like an accident. He's almost gotten away with it, except for his nosy stepdaughter who is terrifyingly like her mother. That nice insurance investigator seemed to be satisfied until Sarah got hold of him. Now she's raising suspicions. What can Arthur do?

In this case the readers will be certain of the details of Millicent's death from the beginning. Because they understand things from Arthur's point of view, they will be rooting for him to find some way out of this mess. They won't care for Sarah and will be hoping that Dan isn't clever enough to figure out what really happened.

Who should your viewpoint character be? It depends upon which story you want to tell. And once you've made that decision, you still have several more to consider: Should you tell your story in the first or third person? Should you view the events in your story objectively or subjectively? And what about using mixed or omniscient viewpoints?

To a certain extent, your choices may be limited by the nature of the story. Some material can only be effectively presented in one particular viewpoint. There are times, however, when you do have a choice. In such instances it is best to write in the viewpoint that feels most comfortable.

Let's take a look at some of the methods of handling the point of view and analyze their strengths and weaknesses.

FIRST-PERSON VIEWPOINT

Nearly all fiction is written in either the first or the third person. Stories written in the first person sound as they they are being told directly by the one who lived through the events in the story. This narrator may be either the protagonist or an observer who describes what happens to the protagonist.

The Narrator/Protagonist

I stopped the car at the entrance to the grounds. The driveway was full of chuckholes big enough to drown a horse. I looked over at Melanie. The poor kid was still blinking back tears. I realized I'd been pretty hard on her.

"Come on, Mel," I said. "We have to walk the rest of the way."

Her legs weren't too steady, so I gripped her arm as we

walked to the main entrance of the house. While I was fumbling in my pocket for the key Reynard had given me, I noticed a bloody fingerprint on the doorknob. The blood was still fresh.

What in hell were we getting into?

I glanced at Melanie, who was dabbing at her eyes with her handkerchief. She was so young. So vulnerable. And she trusted me.

I had to get her out of there.

"Damn!" I muttered. "Would you believe I lost the key? We'll have to go back to town."

This story is being told by the unnamed protagonist. The readers know everything the narrator sees and does *as well as what he knows, thinks, and feels.* Everything is seen subjectively. It is as if the readers were stepping into this person's mind.

There is one great advantage in writing a story this way. Because the readers feel as though they were in the protagonist's mind, the level of reader identification is very high.

On the other hand, you are faced with all those first person pronouns: *I, me,* and *my.* Somehow, the pronouns *he* and *she* never seem to jump off the page the way *I* does. It takes a bit of skill to construct your sentences so that every other one doesn't begin with a first-person pronoun.

Then, too, the entire text must be written in the speech patterns that that character would use. In the foregoing example, the protagonist speaks of "chuckholes big enough to drown a horse." If another character were telling this story, the holes in the driveway might be described differently. For example, Melanie might say, "The driveway was sadly neglected. It was peppered with deep holes."

Keeping the speech patterns consistent with the narrator's character throughout the story helps a great deal in making the readers feel that they are truly inside of someone else's mind, but it takes a lot of concentrated effort. Every sentence must be weighed, not only to see whether or not it says what we want it to say and whether or not it is constructed as well as possible but also to see whether or not it sounds like the narrator speaking.

There is one other subtle drawback to the use of the narrator/protagonist viewpoint, and that is a slight lowering of tension. It comes about because the readers are certain from the outset that the protagonist survived whatever ordeals are being described; otherwise he or she wouldn't be around to tell this story!

The Narrator/Observer

Another method of writing in the first person is that in which the narrator is not the protagonist. The readers are still in the mind of the narrator. They know what he sees and does, thinks, knows, and feels, but the narrator is no longer the chief character in the story. The readers are outside of the protagonist and can only observe him or her.

If this sounds confusing, remember that Sir Arthur Conan Doyle used this viewpoint in his Sherlock Holmes stories. While Holmes is the protagonist, the story is told through the eyes of Dr. Watson and in Dr. Watson's voice.

Reader identification is affected by this technique. The tendency to identify with the narrator is diluted by the fact that the protagonist is a far more interesting character who also invites reader identification.

We have some other limitations as well. Let's return to the previous example and rewrite it in the viewpoint of the narrator/observer. Now the story is being told by a fellow named Rusty who is sitting in the backseat of the car:

> Lucas pulled the car up at the entrance to the grounds. I leaned forward from the backseat and saw why he'd stopped. The driveway was chock full of holes.

In the passenger seat Melanie was still blinking back tears. Lucas looked at her and the lines around his mouth softened. He knew he'd been too hard on her.

"Come on, Mel," he said. "We have to walk the rest of the way." He looked back at me. "You coming, too, Rusty?"

Melanie stumbled and Lucas gripped her arm as we walked to the main entrance of the house. As he fumbled in his pocket for the key Reynard had given him, I saw Lucas stiffen suddenly. I followed his gaze to the doorknob. There was a fresh bloody fingerprint on it.

Lucas frowned and glanced at Melanie, who was dabbing her eyes with her handkerchief again. Then his face relaxed.

"Damn!" he muttered. "Would you believe I lost the key? We'll have to go back to town."

Let's take a look at the necessary differences in writing this scene from the viewpoint of a narrator who is not the protagonist.

The story is still about Lucas. He is the active person and we are interested in what he says and does. But now we are outside of Lucas, looking at events through Rusty's eyes. We can only see what Rusty sees. We even have to lean forward from the backseat to find out why the car has stopped. The driveway is now described in Rusty's words, "chock full of holes."

When Lucas looks at Melanie, we can't know what he's thinking. We can, however, see the lines around his mouth soften and surmise his thoughts. This is what Rusty does: "He knew he'd been too hard on her." In this instance Rusty is correct, but he could as easily be mistaken when he tries to guess what Lucas is thinking. This sometimes offers a nice opportunity to let our readers mislead themselves.

Notice that we cannot say, "Lucas saw the bloody fingerprint." We are limited to what Rusty can see and infer. In this case Rusty sees Lucas stiffen, sees him looking in the

direction of the doorknob, and *concludes* that Lucas is react-
ing to the bloody fingerprint. Such details may seem unnecessarily picky, but remember that our readers are feeling
a certain inclination to identify with Lucas as well as Rusty. If
we accidentally slip into Lucas's point of view from time to
time, the readers will feel manipulated, particularly when
Lucas obviously has information that the narrator doesn't
have.

As you can see, there is a certain artificiality about this
viewpoint and it is best to use it only when necessary. The
best reason for using it is that at a given point in the story, the
protagonist must know more than the reader can be allowed
to know.

THIRD-PERSON VIEWPOINT

This point of view is probably the most popular with both
writers and readers. The narrative is told in the third person,
describing the protagonist as *he* or *she*. The reader may be
either in the protagonist's mind (a subjective view of events)
or looking over the protagonist's shoulder (an objective
view).

Let's go back to our example and see what happens
when it is done in the third person.

Third Person—Subjective View

Lucas stopped the car at the entrance to the grounds.
The driveway was full of chuckholes big enough to
drown a horse.

He looked at Melanie. The poor kid was still blinking
back tears. Maybe he shouldn't have been so hard on
her.

"Come on, Mel. We have to walk the rest of the way."
She was still unsteady, and he gripped her arm as they
walked up to the main entrance of the house.

As he fumbled in his pocket for the key Reynard had
given him, Lucas saw a bloody fingerprint on the
doorknob. The blood was still fresh.

What in hell were they getting into?

He glanced at Melanie who was dabbing her eyes with
her handkerchief again. She was so young. So vulnerable. And she trusted him.

He had to get her out of there.

"Damn!" he muttered. "Would you believe I lost the
key? We'll have to back to town."

If you compare this with the example done in the first person
with a narrator/protagonist, you can see that there is not a
great deal of difference in the material except for the use of
third-person pronouns instead of first. Besides knowing
what Lucas says and does, we know what he knows, thinks,
and feels. Because we are in the protagonist's mind, we have
a high level of reader identification.

On the other hand, one of the drawbacks of telling a
story from a subjective point of view (in the character's mind)
is that the character can't see himself (unless, of course, he's
looking in a mirror), and we can't describe the character as if
the readers were seeing him.

The logic of this seems more obvious in the first person.
Few beginning writers would say:

I ran my fingers through my sandy hair and shrugged
my broad shoulders. There seemed to be no way out.

Yet it is common to find the same illogic in a beginner's
third-person manuscript:

> Lucas ran his fingers through his sandy hair and shrug-
> ged his broad shoulders. There seemed to be no way
> out.

In one sentence the readers are outside of Lucas, looking at
his hair and shoulders. In the next sentence they are inside
his head. Such a change of viewpoint is unsettling, and readers will have trouble identifying with Lucas. They may not
consciously realize that the viewpoint is changing back and
forth, but they will be very aware that something is not quite
right.

By the same logic, when we are writing from a subjective
viewpoint, we cannot say:

> There was a small grease spot on the back of Lucas's
> collar.

Unless, of course, Lucas is doing contortions in front of a
mirror or he has taken the shirt off and is looking at it. If we
need to have the readers know that the spot is there, we
might have Melanie notice it and comment upon it.

Nor can we write such sentences as:

> When Lucas left the house that morning, he forgot to
> take his gun.

Why not? Because when he left the house, he obviously
wasn't aware that he'd forgotten the gun. In the subjective
viewpoint we are limited to know only what he knows, so we
can't be aware that he's forgotten the gun, either.

Similarly, it is unacceptable to write:

> Lucas didn't realize that the elevator had stopped.

or:

Unconsciously, he reached for the telephone.

It takes a little thought to avoid such sentences as these, but after all the work we've gone through to get our readers into the character's mind, it's worth expending a little effort to keep them there.

Whether we are writing in the first person or the third person, one crucial limitation in writing with a subjective point of view is that we cannot fairly withhold any information from the readers if the protagonist has it. Consider the following passage:

> Lucas wondered what he was going to do. There wasn't much time.
>
> The phone rang. Inspector Holloway was on the line. Lucas listened grimly. When he replaced the receiver, he turned to Melanie.
>
> "I've got to leave for a while. Lock the place up tight and don't let anyone in!"

Until now, our readers have been in Lucas's mind, sharing his thoughts and feelings. But as soon as we say *Lucas listened grimly* without saying what he heard, we have cheated. In effect, we are saying to the readers, "Now Lucas is getting a piece of information that I'll tell you about later." Our readers are suddenly aware that they are not in Lucas's mind after all. The fantasy has been shattered. The result is disappointment.

Occasionally, under certain conditions, an author can get away with withholding information. (See the discussion on breaking the rules in Chapter 15.) However, in general, when you find that your protagonist must logically have information that cannot be shared with the readers immediately, you should consider changing your viewpoint so that your protagonist is seen objectively.

In this viewpoint the story is told as if the readers were watching the main character in much the same way that they might watch a character in the movies or on television. They know what the protagonist does and says and what happens to him, but they cannot enter his mind.

The passage describing Lucas and Melanie arriving at the house might now go like this:

> Lucas stopped the car at the entrance to the grounds. The driveway was full of potholes.
>
> He looked at Melanie. She was still blinking back tears. He reached over and squeezed her hand. "Come on, Mel. We've got to walk the rest of the way."
>
> She stumbled and he gripped her arm as they walked up to the main entrance of the house. As he fumbled in his pocket for the key Reynard had given him, Lucas's gaze fell upon the doorknob. There was a bloody fingerprint on it, and the blood was still fresh.
>
> He glanced at Melanie, who was dabbing her eyes with her handkerchief again.
>
> "Damn!" he muttered. "Would you believe I lost the key? We'll have to go back to town."

Notice that the description of the driveway is now strictly objective. Rather than describing it in the way that Lucas would, we are simply conveying the facts to the readers.

We show that Lucas feels sympathy for Melanie by having him reach over and squeeze her hand. We cannot show that he regrets any earlier actions unless he *says* so. The readers have to interpret Lucas's motives from his speech and actions. Thus, we have to be certain that his speech and actions clearly reveal everything we want our readers to know.

Because we are not inside the protagonist's mind, reader identification is lowered, and it is best to compensate for this by having plenty of action and drama.

From a practical stance, the third-person objective viewpoint often serves nicely for a short piece, but it is difficult to write an entire book from that viewpoint because of the stringent limitations on the author. It can be done, however; Gregory McDonald does it very effectively in his Fletch novels.

MIXED VIEWPOINT

Some stories are best told from the viewpoint of more than one character. To insure that the readers feel neither confused nor manipulated, it is a good idea to compartmentalize the book. For example, we might change viewpoints with each chapter. Or we might divide the book or the chapters into sections, each in a particular viewpoint. Within a chapter or a section, however, the viewpoint should be consistent.

We are still bound by the same rules as before: when we are in Lucas's mind, we are limited to what he knows and we may not withhold any information he has. When we switch to Melanie's mind, we know what is going on in her mind but not in his.

If you are writing a whodunit using several viewpoints, you may unwittingly be eliminating a number of possible suspects because once the murder has been committed, we cannot enter the mind of the murderer without knowing it.

When Agatha Christie wrote *The Murder of Roger Ackroyd*, some critics argued that she had violated this principle. A thoughtful reading, however, will show that she did not.

On the other hand, a superb unconventional mystery that uses mixed viewpoint, one of which *is* that of the murderer, is Ira Levin's *A Kiss Before Dying*. It is worth studying to see the skillful use of mixed viewpoint.

As a rule, reader identification is quite low with a mixed viewpoint, and it helps if you have one viewpoint that is more prominent than the others.

It also helps if the connections between the various viewpoint characters are made clear before the story is too far underway. The readers shouldn't have to wonder whether they are still reading the same story.

OMNISCIENT VIEWPOINT

In this viewpoint the author is free to put the readers inside anyone's mind at will. Furthermore, the author can state facts that none of the characters are aware of.

> Laura Anderson poured another cup of coffee for Harold. If only it hadn't rained again! She had wanted to go shopping so badly.

> Harold folded his paper and sniffed in self-pity. Damn cold! It was the worst time of year to have a cold, too.

> Half a mile to the rear of the Anderson house, the crack in the dam to the Hammond Reservoir grew wider.

In the truly omniscient viewpoint, reader identification is quite low. Also, any information that is withheld from the readers is withheld arbitrarily by the author. Thus, there is the danger that the readers may feel cheated. In general, it takes an intricately plotted story to compensate for these potential problems, and conventional mysteries are not often written in the omniscient viewpoint.

However, long, complex suspense novels often lend themselves to this treatment. In such stories there are usually a number of characters plotting at cross purposes, and suspense is derived from the fact that the readers know more than any one of them and can foresee possible consequences. Suspense is also kept high because there are several problems being dealt with and at any given time somebody is in deep trouble. Ken Follett's *The Eye of the Needle* and Frederick Forsyth's *The Odessa File* are good examples of writing in the omniscient viewpoint.

OTHER USES OF VIEWPOINT

Emotional Coloring

Careful use of viewpoint can be effective for directing readers' suspicions in the mystery. To illustrate, let's look at a passage in the third-person subjective view:

> Simon found Iris in the gallery. The poor child was crying. "Here." He offered her his handkerchief. "Let's sit by the fire for a while, shall we?"

Iris is being seen through Simon's eyes. He feels sorry for her, and the readers are invited to feel sorry for her, too. This can be useful if we don't want the readers to consider Iris a likely suspect at this point.

In the same way we can use Simon's emotions to sway the readers against a character.

> Ruby came down the stairs, her eyes still swollen from crying. Simon wondered whether she always used tears to get her way. She'd been doing enough of that this weekend!
>
> "I suppose you think I'm wrong," she said softly.
>
> "I think," Simon said, looking her in the eye, "that you should grow up."

Our readers are not likely to care very much for Ruby because Simon—through whose eyes they are seeing things—doesn't like her.

Misinterpretation by the Viewpoint Character

If our readers are seeing events through a character's eyes, it is not unfairly misleading the readers if that character misinterprets what he sees.

> As Simon approached the main house, he saw Alex struggling with the key to the front door. "I'm glad you've come home," Simon said as he mounted the steps. "I have to ask your mother some questions. I'd prefer you to be there."
>
> "Of course." Alex held the door for him. "Mother! I'm home!" His voice rang hollowly in the large hall. There was no reply.
>
> "Perhaps she's napping," Simon said.
>
> "She doesn't usually." Alex pushed open the door to the library and froze. "Oh, my God!"
>
> Mrs. Renfield lay in a pool of blood by the hearth.

At this point, Simon won't suspect Alex because it appears that Alex only just arrived. But that is really an assumption on Simon's part. If, later in the book Simon realizes that Alex could just as well have been *locking* the door on his way *out* of the house, our readers will wonder why they didn't realize that themselves.

We have not misled them. We showed them what Simon saw and told them how Simon interpreted it. It is up to the readers to realize that Simon's interpretation is not necessarily the correct one.

Pointing Out a Significant Thought

The first-person viewpoint is sometimes used to distinguish thoughts from speech in a narrative that is otherwise third-person. When combined with the use of italics, it is particularly useful to make sure the readers realize the significance of the thought. This technique is most often used in the following situations:

1. *When a character is remembering a statement to which you want to call the readers' attention.* This is a handy way to remind the readers of something that may have been said several chapters earlier or that may have been passed over lightly at the time and has now taken on a new significance.

> As Lucas helped Melanie into the car, his mind was on that bloody fingerprint. They said Waldo had been wounded in the prison break.
>
> *I'm going to get those Harringtons for what they did to me. Every last one of them!*
>
> Lucas slid behind the wheel and gripped it tightly. Melanie *was* the last Harrington.

Here we are reminding the readers that Waldo threatened Melanie's entire family. These are words the readers have seen before. Because they are quoted exactly, in the first person, and italicized, great importance will now be attached to them.

Compare the lesser impact of reminding the readers of the same threat by simply giving them the necessary information:

> Lucas remembered that Waldo had threatened the entire Harrington family at the time of his conviction.

The same technique is useful in another situation:

2. *When the character is making an important unspoken promise to himself or to someone else.* In this case, we want to point out the character's motives to make sure that the readers understand we are dealing with a matter of importance.

> Lucas released the brake and backed the car onto the road.
>
> *Don't worry, Mel. I'm going to get you out of this if it's the last thing I do. I promised your father I'd take care of you.*
>
> He smiled at her. "Are you all right?"
>
> She nodded.

The use of first person and italics makes Lucas's resolve appear far stronger and more dramatic than if it were simply stated directly:

> Lucas released the brake and backed the car onto the road. He had to get Melanie out of this, if it was the last thing he ever did. He'd promised her father.
>
> He smiled at her. "Are you all right?"
>
> She nodded.

SUMMARY

The skillful use of viewpoint can aid reader identification with the protagonist, explain the protagonist's motives, maintain a logical sequence of information that is to be given to the readers, lend emotional coloring to the events in your story, and help the readers appreciate the significance of certain thoughts.

Obviously, the selection of a viewpoint from which to tell a story is not one that should be made lightly. And until you have mastered the art of handling viewpoints, it is a good idea to check your manuscript sentence by sentence to be sure that you are being consistent and that you are viewing events from the best possible perspective.

8
Researching

One of the basic rules of writing is to write what you know. It makes sense. Writing is communicating and you can't communicate what you don't know.

Furthermore, writing fiction is more than giving the readers information. It is creating another world and inviting the readers to enter it and experience certain events.

And writing mystery and suspense fiction is different from writing other types of fiction in this way: Though it is possible to enjoy some novels that are read with a certain amount of detachment, there is no such thing as a good mystery that allows detachment on the part of the readers. The better the mystery is, the higher the percentage of readers who say, "I couldn't put it down!"

Thus, any detail that makes your fictional world seem real to your readers helps to keep them involved in your story. Likewise, any detail that strikes the readers as inaccurate, inappropriate, or implausible tends to jar them. A small inaccuracy may cause a slight detachment, but a glaring mistake can cause them to put your book down in disgust. And, thanks to the mass media, readers today are better informed than ever.

Therefore, it is best to write about things that you know well. And if you need to write about something you don't know well, you had better do some research.

If you want to write mysteries, you will need to be thoroughly familiar with correct procedures in criminal investigation because, thanks to television, most of your readers will know something about them. You can assume your readers know quite a bit about fingerprinting, identifying footprints and tire marks, matching bullets with the guns from which they were fired, and what information can be acquired from bits of hair, fibers, metal particles or samples of blood, saliva, or semen.

But what about other areas? How do you decide whether or not you need to do research on a given point?

WHEN DO YOU NEED
TO DO RESEARCH?

Suppose you are going to have your protagonist in a restaurant, eating dinner with Barney, who is suddenly striken by a heart attack. If you've never seen anyone have a heart attack, you probably need to research the matter.

There is always the temptation to rationalize: You've seen a lot of heart attacks depicted on television or in the movies. There's nothing to it. The actor simply groans and clutches his chest and keels over. Why can't you do the same thing in fiction?

Well, try it:

> As I helped myself to another muffin, Barney groaned. Suddenly he clutched his chest and keeled over.
>
> I stood up and shouted, "Somebody call an ambulance!"

What went wrong? It happened that quickly on television. Why can't we do it as quickly on paper?

Think about it. When you watched that character on television, you saw a thousand little details at once. You saw whether he clutched his chest with one hand or two, whether he fell forward, backward, or sideways. You saw whether he knocked his glass of water over, whether he was unconscious afterward. Did he try to speak? If he did, could he actually say anything understandable, or did he just groan and gasp? And although you may not remember whether he was pale or flushed, perspiring or not, you *did* see his face.

And if this was a halfway believable production, the actor didn't fall to the floor without some preliminary indications that something was wrong. He may have loosened his collar or his belt because a person who is experiencing a heart attack feels constricted. He may have mopped his brow with a handkerchief or removed his jacket, because perspiration and a clammy feeling are symptoms of a heart attack. And though you may not consciously remember seeing all these details, you *saw* them. And they helped to make that heart attack seem real.

Now look at what you put on paper. What did your readers see? Almost nothing. A picture is truly worth a thousand words, and you are faced with finding the right ones. You have to give the readers enough details to make the experience seem real and they have to be accurate. If you want to describe Barney's face, you have to *know* whether it's likely to be flushed or pale. What kind of an expression might he have?

And another thing: Even if you *did* witness someone having a heart attack, you need to know whether or not it was a typical one. If your Uncle Jake had a mild heart attack on Wednesday and danced a jig on the following Saturday, you had best not offer that as a normal recovery from a heart attack. No matter that it actually happened.

HOW MUCH RESEARCH
DO YOU NEED TO DO?

How much research is needed? It will depend upon the part that special information plays in your story. If your readers are seeing everything through the eyes of your protagonist (let's call him Jack) and Jack is with Barney for some time before he has the heart attack, you'll need to know what indications of the impending attack Jack might have noticed.

What happens when help arrives? Will we see ambulance attendants or paramedics or both? And what will they do when they come?

If Jack goes with Barney to the hospital, you have to know what will be done in the ambulance on the way and what happens when they get to the hospital. Is the heart specialist likely to be on hand, or will there be a delay? Who does what in the meantime? Will Barney get any medication? Will they hook him up to any kind of special equipment?

And where will Jack be during all of this? Outside the emergency room, looking through a little window in the door? (*Is* there a little window in the door?) Or will he have to wait in a visitor's area? What does the visitor's area look like? Who will keep Jack informed as to Barney's condition? How long is Barney likely to be in the emergency room? And where does he go from there?

On the other hand, if Jack doesn't go to the hospital for one reason or another, you only need to know what he sees happening up to the point where Jack and Barney part company. In other words, you won't need to know a lot of details about the hospital procedures. You might, however, want to know how long Barney is likely to be in the hospital, whether or not Jack will be allowed to see him if he chooses to do so, and what happens when Barney is released, if that's going to be part of the story.

A good rule to follow is to find out more than you think you'll need for your story. You can always discard material if you don't need it, but you can't be certain that your preconceived ideas are accurate until you check them.

At this point, a lot of beginning writers get discouraged. Where on earth do you find the answers to all those questions?

FORMAL SOURCES OF INFORMATION

Your Personal Library

Some professional writers have enormous collections of books. Obviously, it saves a lot of time and energy to have references at your fingertips instead of having to trot down to the public library every time you need a bit of information.

It isn't really necessary to go out and buy a lot of books, however. If you choose your books carefully, you can build a small but efficient personal library that will serve most of your daily writing needs. What kind of books should you have?

You ought to have a good dictionary or two, a basic text on English grammar, a thesaurus, an atlas, a recent almanac, and a book of names. An inexpensive condensed encyclopedia can be helpful, as can a basic text in United States history, a Bible, a book of quotations, and a book on mythology. Particularly helpful are texts in psychology—at least one in general psychology and one in abnormal psychology. Guides to prescription and nonprescription drugs, their uses and side effects, are invaluable. So are introductory texts on criminal investigation and forensic examination of evidence.

And if your protagonist is an expert in some other area—say, she's an art collector—you ought to have some good reference material on the subject.

If you like to use foreign settings, a subscription to *National Geographic* is a good investment, as are language guides for travelers.

As you continue to write, you will find that your reference needs will be more clearly defined. And all those textbooks need not cost you a fortune, either. College bookstores usually sell used texts for a fraction of the original price. Library book sales offer another opportunity to pick up reference books cheaply. And, of course, if you have a public library nearby, you needn't invest in expensive reference books you'll only need once in a while.

The Public Library

The public library probably contains the greatest collection of information to which you have easy access. Learn to use it. Even if your local library is not large, you still may be able to use it to acquire books from other libraries in the area. Unless your story deals with a great deal of specialized information, most of the material you need can be found here.

Specialty Libraries

If you live near a college or university, you may have access to a number of specialty libraries—libraries of medicine, art, geology, and so on. In some cases you may be able to use such libraries freely. In others you may have to get special permission or pay a fee if you are not a student.

Museums

From the large museums of science, natural history, and fine arts to the small ones run by local historical societies and special-interest groups, museums are treasure troves of information. Do you need to know about voodoo, the circus, or medieval armor? You may have access to museums specializing in those subjects. And if you don't live near the museum you are interested in, you can write to it for specific information. Start in the reference department of your local library, where you should find one or more of the following:

Herbert and Marjorie Katz. *Museums USA—A History and Guide.* New York: Doubleday, 1965.

Kenneth Hudson and Ann Nicholls. *The Directory of World Museums.* New York: Columbia University Press, 1975.

American Association of Museums. *The Official Museum Directory 1981.* Skokie, Ill.: National Register Publishing Co., 1981.

The Government Printing Office

The U.S. Government Printing Office publishes documents on almost every subject imaginable. For a nominal sum you can order such treasures as a handbook compiled by the FBI on the uses and classification of fingerprints, or a forensic handbook that describes official methods of collecting and handling evidence. You can get publications on law, poisons, drugs, or firearms, all of which are particularly helpful to a crime writer.

Most public libraries will have the monthly catalog of U.S. government publications in the reference department. You can also write directly to the Superintendent of Documents, U.S. Government Printing Office, Washington, D.C. 20402.

Special-Interest Organizations

Do you need to know a lot about alcoholism or child abuse? How about the symptoms of rheumatoid arthritis or of drug addition? What problems face a person living with a compulsive gambler? How will a seeing-eye dog react if a stranger breaks into a house and pulls a gun?

There are nonprofit organizations specializing in each of these areas, and you can get a lot of information from them for the asking.

Do you need to know something about ham radios, hot-air balloons, mountain climbing, antique autos, or spelunking? There are clubs dedicated to these interests. It may take a bit of detective work on your part to find them, however. Begin with the telephone directory and the reference department of the library.

Special-Interest Publications

Suppose you need information on guns or ammunition, rare coins, stamps, ceramics, or old bottles. If someone collects it, there's probably a magazine devoted to the subject.

Don't overlook professional and hobby magazines, either. Suppose your protagonist is going to own a dry cleaning shop, an amusement park, a pharmacy, or a buffalo farm? In each case, there's a magazine devoted to the interests of that business. If she's going to be a pilot, a skier, a golfer, a horse enthusiast, or a gymnast, there's a magazine on the subject. If he's a fisherman, a hot-rodder, or a treasure hunter, there's a magazine devoted to each of those subjects, too.

If your library doesn't have a copy of the publication you are interested in and you can't get it at a newsstand, you may have to write to the publisher. You can get the address from *The Writer's Market* or *The Writer's Handbook*, which should be in the reference department of the library.

Police Agencies

Your city, county, and state police and the local office of the FBI can often be helpful with technical questions. Most police departments will have a public-relations office you can contact.

Open Houses and Special Demonstrations

Police departments, fire departments, and hospitals often have open houses and demonstrations where you can pick up handy information on various subjects, such as the use of dogs to sniff out bombs, cardiopulmonary resuscitation, and the latest laboratory equipment available for detecting poisons in the blood.

If you have the opportunity to visit Washington, D.C., be sure to take the tour of the FBI Building and see their laboratories, historical memorabilia, and firearms collection and demonstration.

Businesses

Do you need to know a lot about the paper industry or how the telephone company functions? Most large businesses have a public relations department. Many even offer guided tours of their facilities.

Newspaper Files

Your local library will probably have several years worth of local newspapers, either bound or on microfilm. If you need to go back further than that, the newspaper itself has its own files, which are generally open to the public.

Travel Agencies

If your character is in an unfamiliar setting or is doing any traveling in your story, a travel agency or tourist bureau can often provide helpful information. Brochures with colorful photographs and schedules for planes, trains, buses, ships, and ferries are available, along with information on such subjects as normal daily temperatures and currency exchange.

Interviewing

Let's go back to that scene in which Barney has a heart attack. Suppose you've decided that you are going to have paramedics attend him. If there is a paramedic unit near where you live, it may be helpful to talk with them in person. These people, like most dedicated professionals, are generally very happy to talk about their work with someone who is truly interested.

One word of caution, however. If you want to conduct an interview, even a short informal one, don't drop in out of the blue and expect someone to take time from work to show you around and answer questions. If you have only a few specific questions that could be answered in a half hour or so, call ahead. Explain who you are and that you are writing a story or a book in which paramedics appear. Say that you'd like to be able to talk with someone who can make sure your details are accurate.

Few people will resist such an approach. Be sure to have your questions prepared in advance. This not only saves time, but it can avoid the need to call back for additional information. Sometimes, of course, you will need to return to ask a few more questions, but if it happens too often, you'll get a reputation as "that pesky writer," and you'll find that doors are not opening as easily as they used to when you ask for an interview.

What happens when you need a lot of specialized information from an interview? Suppose you're writing a novel in which the protagonist is a paramedic who suspects that some of the "accidents" he is called to aren't really accidents.

Now you want to know a lot more than what a paramedic does when he's called to give emergency treatment to an individual heart attack victim. You have to learn what the daily routine of a paramedic is like. What training is needed to become a paramedic? What procedures are followed for various emergencies?

You need to know what the inside of the fire station is like, as well as the inside of the paramedics' van, and the inside of the ambulance and the emergency ward. What kind of terminology do they use? What kind of equipment do they take with them? What is each article called, and what is it used for? You'll have hundreds of questions.

Obviously, you will be asking for a great deal of someone's time and attention. Whether or not you can get it may depend upon how you go about trying to get it.

The first thing you should do is find out as much as you can on your own. Start with the library and track down as many other sources of public information as you can. There are three reasons for doing such preliminary work: First of all, you have a better sense of the questions you need to ask. You won't be wasting a professional person's time asking questions you could easily have answered yourself. Second, people are far more willing to cooperate with someone who appears serious about the project at hand. If you act like a pro, you'll be treated like one. Third, it is difficult to explain technical matters to someone who knows nothing about the subject. If you are perceived as an amateur who has only a passing interest in the material at hand, your questions will be answered with far fewer details—details that could make a great difference in your book.

The next thing to do is to write a businesslike letter, explaining the kind of book you are writing (you need not go into the plot; simply say that the main character will be a paramedic and a lot of the story has to do with paramedical work). Request permission to observe procedures and routines at the station and to interview a specific person or the unit in general. The letter should go to the public relations department, if there is one, or to the person in charge—that is, the boss of the people you wish to interview. As much as possible, be flexible as to the time or times of the interviews. People are more cooperative when things are done at their convenience.

The third thing to do is to be on time. Have your questions ready, and be attentive to the answers offered you. If you are left waiting for periods of time, use the opportunity to observe the details that will go into your setting and make notes of what is going on around you. It may be helpful to take photographs, but be sure to get permission first.

Above all, don't interfere with anyone's work. If you sense that you're wearing out your welcome, call it a day, even if you haven't yet go everything you hoped to get. Part of the art of interviewing is to make the interviewee feel comfortable about having you around so that you can observe him or her behaving as naturally as possible.

Interviewing can be an enjoyable and educational experience. You'll be meeting interesting people doing interesting things. Sometimes there's even a double payoff, for often an interview for one story will generate ideas for another.

INFORMAL SOURCES OF INFORMATION

If all this sounds as though a writer must spend half his life in libraries, take heart. A lot of information gathering can be done in a casual manner during your normal daily activities.

Are you going shopping in a department store? Start reading the labels in clothing. Pretty soon you'll be able to tell at a glance the difference between an all-wool suit and a rayon blend, between a cotton skirt and a linen one, between velvet and velveteen.

Pay attention to styles, particularly those that won't date your story. Some things never seem to be out of style. It is best to dress your characters in such clothes whenever you need to describe their apparel in detail. (Unless, of course, your story is taking place at a specific time in history.)

And when you have a chance to browse, don't stop with the clothing department. Learn a little about basic furniture styles. Your indoor scenes will be more effective if your readers see a teal blue wing chair and a Queen Anne desk instead of a blue chair and a desk.

Going out to eat? Order something you've never eaten before. Pay attention to what it looks like and how it tastes. The next time one of your characters has dinner, you'll have an interesting dish to put on the table.

Even if you don't garden, you can pick up a lot about the subject by reading the garden section of your local newspaper or following the garden expert on the radio. As a result, your protagonist's neighbor won't simply be tending her flowers; she'll be dusting her roses to protect them from Japanese beetles.

And the next time you take your car in for repairs, ask the mechanic exactly what was wrong. Pay attention to the terminology he uses. Now your character won't merely have a squeak in his car; he'll have a loose fan belt or a worn universal joint.

When you're away from home, don't miss the opportunity to gather information on a possible setting for a future story. Save travel brochures and tour guide information. Make notes of interesting details that aren't likely to be found in the travel books at the library.

If you make a general habit of being observant and inquisitive, you'll find a wealth of information all around you. The little details that you accumulate will eventually find their way into your writing, making it vivid and more interesting.

9

Style and Tone

What is style? One thing is sure: Good writers have it. Beginning writers often worry about it and try to develop it by imitating good writers. Unfortunately, this only results in imitations of good writing. Would you pick up a book that was labeled "An imitation Raymond Chandler novel"? You'd want the real thing, wouldn't you?

Style *is* the real thing. In order to be a good writer, you must develop your *own* method of putting words together to convey your ideas.

How does one go about developing a style? It comes naturally with practice (lots of it!) and from an awareness of what good writing does.

There are plenty of books on writing available, and the subject cannot be covered in great depth in a single chapter here. But basically there are three questions to keep in mind when you write:

1. What exactly do I want to say?
2. How can I say it most clearly?
3. How can I say it most effectively?

Knowing Exactly What You Want to Say

It may seem overly fundamental to say that you have to know what information you wish to communicate before you can do so. Yet, many inexperienced writers attempt to put on paper thoughts that are not completely formed. The result is vague and confusing to the readers. How can they know what you are trying to say if you aren't sure yourself?

Be specific. Watch out for vague or general terms. Remember that one word can conjure up a range of images among your readers.

> The dead woman was named Monica Jackman. She had been a successful young singer who lived just outside of Los Angeles.

Some of your readers will figure that Monica was a successful singer if she managed to make a living by singing. Others will imagine that she made a million dollars a year. *Successful* is a relative term. So is *young*. Some readers will imagine that Monica was sixteen. Others will figure she's somewhere under thirty-five. The important thing is: What do *you* mean?

If Monica is an eighteen-year-old who owns a mansion in Beverly Hills, three Rolls Royces, and a Lear jet, say so.

On the other hand, if she's twenty-nine and owns a Cadillac and a well-furnished condominium in Pasadena, say that.

Avoid excess adverbs and adjectives. A good habit to get into is to be wary of adjectives and adverbs. Too often, they are used to disguise fuzzy thinking and laziness on the part of the author. Look at the following sentence:

> Catherine went as quietly as she could into the kitchen
> and carefully took a large sharp knife from the drawer
> where all the knives were kept.

Now let's say that more efficiently:

> Catherine crept into the kitchen and slipped a butcher
> knife from the cutlery drawer.

We've cut the number of words from twenty-six to four-
teen and sharpened the mental images we are presenting.
Different readers will imagine different knives when they
come to the words *a large sharp knife*. But *a butcher knife* will
evoke a pretty standard image.

In the same way, when we say *Catherine crept* we are
telling the readers more than when we say *Catherine went as
quietly as she could*. *Crept* implies an air of furtiveness that is
not expressed in *went as quietly as she could*. The same thing
happens with *slipped* and *carefully took*.

Learn to make each word do as much as possible. One of
the ways to do this is to use specific nouns and verbs. For
example, *went* is a general verb. Even with five modifiers, it
could not tell the readers as much as the specific verb *crept*.

Writing Clearly

It is one thing to know what you want to say and another to
convey that idea to your readers. When you are telling a
story, the meaning of each sentence must be clear. Your
readers cannot ask you to explain what you mean. And if
your readers are not sure what you mean, they are likely to
put your book down—permanently.

Consider:

> Inspector Drake established that Jack only handled the
> murder weapon.

There is nothing grammatically incorrect about this sentence, but it is not clear what the author is trying to say. Since *only* can mean either *alone* or *merely*, the implication of this sentence could be either that Jack *must* be the murderer (since he alone handled the murder weapon), or that he *cannot* be the murderer (since he merely handled the weapon; he did not *use* it).

Carelessly placed modifiers frequently cause confusion. In the foregoing sentence, the placement of the word *only* creates the problem. But a badly handled phrase can also obscure the meaning of a sentence:

> Jessica's body was lying on the carpet in the corner of the study.

Strictly speaking, this sentence says that the carpet was in the corner of the study and Jessica's body was lying on it. But since carpets are not usually confined to corners of rooms (unless they are rolled up, perhaps to be taken out for cleaning), the sentence presents a confusing image. If it is necessary to emphasize that the body is not lying on a bare floor, it would be clearer to say:

> Jessica's body lay in the corner of the study. The blood from the wound in her neck had soaked into the carpet.

Now there is no ambiguity.

Modifying phrases incorrectly placed sometimes result in absurd sentences:

> The policeman with the large belly's gun remained on the table. (The policeman with the large belly left his gun on the table.)

> Having been dead for more than ten years, we didn't remember Mrs. Higgins very well.

This last sentence actually says that we have been dead for more than ten years. Clearly, that is not what the author meant to say. These examples are ludicrous and the problems are therefore easy to spot. Sometimes, however, it isn't that simple. For example, you might write:

My brother Seymour is coming to dinner.

but not:

My wife, Louise, is roasting a turkey.

Why not? Unless you mean to tell your readers that the narrator is a bigamist, the latter sentence should be:

My wife, Louisie, is roasting a turkey.

In order to be certain that you are indeed saying what you mean, it's a good idea to keep a basic text in English grammar handy and to refer to it often.

Be aware of connotations.
A connotation is an implied meaning as opposed to a literal one.

Holly was one of Harry's slenderest models.
Noel was one of Harry's skinniest models.

Skinny and *slender* have the same literal meaning, but because they have different connotations, we are being flattering to Holly and unflattering to Noel while saying the same thing about both women.

Problems with connotations also arise when a word or phrase has different meanings in different situations:

Phillip, an overworked executive, looked upon the mountain cabin as a retreat.

The meaning of that sentence is clear. Phillip welcomes the chance to go to the cabin and escape from the pressures of work. But suppose we say:

Lloyd, a brigadier general, looked upon the mountain cabin as a retreat.

Now some confusion arises. In military terms, the word *retreat* often has unfavorable connotations. Does Lloyd like to go to the cabin or not? It isn't clear, and the sentence should be rewritten.

Sometimes confusion between the connotation and the literal meaning produces unintentional humor:

James and his brothers all liked pullover sweaters. They were a close-knit family.

If such a play on words creeps unnoticed into your story, it can destroy the tension and suspense you are working hard to create.

Other sources of confusion. At times a sentence may be absolutely correct grammatically and yet cause temporary confusion to your readers because of the physical difficulty of reading the sentence. The most common causes of this problem are:

1. *Using different meanings of the same word.*

She picked up a pencil and pencilled in the name of the suspects.

It wasn't fair to go to the fair on Tuesday, even if it was the only day when the weather was fair.

2. *Using homonyms or similar-sounding words.*

> Didn't you warn her about the coat he'd worn?
>
> He killed the cat and put it into the kiln.

3. *Using words that have the same or similar spelling.*

> As I wiped a tear from her cheek, I noticed a tear in her skirt.
>
> The neighborhood patrolmen patronize this store.

4. *Using too much alliteration.*

> Stewart slowly stepped into the stillness of the study.

In the foregoing examples, confusion arises because the eye catches similarities in the appearance of certain words, or the ear catches similarities in sounds. The brain must do a double take at the realization that those words have unexpected meanings. It may take only a fraction of a second for the readers to make that mental adjustment, but that is often enough to jar them out of our fictional world.

The English language is rich with synonyms, and it is easy to avoid confusion generated by the appearance or the sound of words. It takes only a bit of care.

Writing Effectively

It is possible to write clearly with varying degrees of effectiveness. Consider:

> There was nothing on the table.

There is no mistaking the meaning of that sentence. It is clear. But it could be written more effectively. Because of the structure of the sentence, the word which impresses the readers as most important is *nothing*.

But what kind of an image is evoked by a word such as *nothing*? The readers draw a blank. The word *table*, as the object of the prepositional phrase, is in a weak position in this sentence and it cannot evoke a strong image, either. Consequently, we are giving the readers information only.

The chief principle of effective writing is: *Present the readers with strong images.*

Let's rewrite that sentence:

The table was bare.

In this version, the sentence has two strong words, *table* and *bare*. Now our readers are more likely to visualize a table and "see" that it is bare.

Obviously, the importance attached to a word depends partly upon its position in the sentence. Consider these two examples:

A small silver clock chimed happily from the mantle.

From the mantle, a small silver clock chimed happily.

The first sentence focuses attention on the clock itself. The second sentence puts the clock into the background. Which sentence would you use if the clock will later be important to your plot?

This doesn't necessarily mean that important words must always come at the beginning of the sentence. Sometimes it is more effective to put them at the very end:

In the center of the room, amid broken vases and torn curtains, triumphant upon a heap of cushions that belonged on the sofa, sat a white miniature poodle.

Another way to make your images stronger is to *use verbs effectively*. Compare these sentences:

Jeremy was in the den.

Jeremy sat in the den.

Which gives our readers a clearer picture of Jeremy? The second, obviously, because it specifies not only his location but what he is doing. Our readers can picture Jeremy easier if we show them his physical attitude.

Sometimes, it may suit our purpose to show his mental attitude:

Jeremy waited in the den.

Now, even though our readers cannot be certain whether he is sitting or standing, they do know Jeremy's state of mind, and that helps them to picture him more clearly. If they visualize him standing, they may imagine that he has his hands clasped behind his back. If they visualize him sitting, they may imagine him drumming his fingers on the arm of his chair.

In the best of all possible worlds, we will choose a verb that defines both his physical and his mental attitude. Usually, this will be a verb showing *motion*.

Jeremy paced the floor in the den.

Now, not only do our readers see what Jeremy is doing and understand what he is feeling, but their image of him is all the stronger because they are seeing him *in action*.

It is easier to identify with someone you have seen in a motion picture than with someone you have seen only in still photographs. The same principle holds in fiction. Readers find our characters more real and more interesting when we show them in action.

Sometimes, of course, our characters must be motionless. But even then some verb forms are more effective than others. In particular, the simple past tense is usually a better choice than the imperfect past tense. Thus:

Mabel was lying on the sofa.

becomes

Mabel lay on the sofa.

It is true that as far as informational content goes, these two sentences are the same. However, their effects on the readers are quite different. When we say *Mabel was lying on the sofa*, the readers feel they are being told. But when we say *Mabel lay on the sofa*, they feel they are being shown. The simple past tense produces the stronger image.

Similarly, sentences that begin *There was* . . . or *There were* . . . convey the feeling of being told. Whenever possible, convert these into more active sentences.

There was a bloodstain on the pillow.

becomes

Blood stained the pillow.

Strong images are also formed by positive statements rather than negative ones.

Esther was not an outgoing woman.

becomes

Esther was a quiet woman.

Parsonville was not a large town.

becomes

Parsonville was a small town.

or

> Parsonville was a medium-size town.

The principle is simple: It is easier to visualize what a thing or a person is than what it is not.

TONE—A REFLECTION OF ATTITUDE

After you have decided what you want to say and how to say it clearly and effectively, you still need to consider one more question: How do I want my readers to feel?

Usually, you will have to worry about two kinds of feelings in your story. The first is caused by the situation at hand. The second is related to the person through whose eyes we are seeing things.

For example, being trapped in a burning house is a frightening situation for anyone. But it will be different for a professional firefighter than for a paraplegic. These two people have different options available and have the benefit of different experiences.

The firefighter is trained for this situation, and he has the use of his legs. On the other hand, maybe the paraplegic has faced death before. Perhaps he lived very near it for a long time and can view his present situation in an almost detached manner. And because his legs are useless, he has built up the strength in his arms to an extraordinary degree.

Even if both men escape the fire through their own ingenuity, they will probably have very different attitudes toward what has happened.

The tone of your story is a reflection of attitude; it may be yours or that of your protagonist or a combination of both. The important thing is that the tone of the story remain consistent throughout.

It is easiest to maintain such consistency if your story is told from a single viewpoint. Whether your protagonist is miserable or ecstatic, relaxed or terrified, there should be a certain uniformity in his or her outlook. Your readers must never doubt that they are seeing the same person on page 242 that they met on page 1. This doesn't mean that a character can't change in the course of a book, but the change must be gradual and consistent with events in the story.

If you are telling a story from a multiple viewpoint, there will be some variation in tone as the readers see the world through the eyes of different characters who must necessarily have differing attitudes. However—and this is important—the book *as a whole* must have a tone that is consistent.

(If this seems to be an impossibility, read Dorothy Gilman's *The Unexpected Mrs. Pollifax*, in which a widowed grandmother volunteers to be a spy for the CIA. In the course of the book Mrs. Pollifax finds herself in several life-threatening situations that, in themselves, are not at all funny. And yet—even with changes of viewpoint—the over-all tone of the book is consistently lighthearted and amusing. Here the tone results partly from Mrs. Pollifax's attitude and partly from the author's.)

Once you've selected the tone you want to establish, try to get yourself into a frame of mind that reflects it. Feel what you want your readers to feel. This is important, for the words you select and the structure of the sentences you write will depend upon the attitude you have at the time of writing. The trick is to maintain the same attitude throughout the writing of the story.

That might not be hard to do with a short story, but a novel can take months—even years. Is it possible to stay in the same frame of mind for so long? Of course not. What you must learn to do is to get back into the same attitude each time you approach the typewriter. One way to do this is to reread what you wrote at the last sitting. On some days, of course, you'll do better than on others, and on a good day you may want to rework parts that were written on a bad day.

Some authors have personal tricks to help them get into the proper frame of mind for writing. One may have a favorite article of clothing that is always worn during writing sessions. Another has a certain selection of music to be played in the background. Most say a regular writing schedule is a great help.

Eventually, with practice, it will become easier to slip into an appropriate attitude. Good writers are like good actors in that respect. They study feelings, try them on for size, analyze them, and learn to be comfortable with them. For only then is the actor—or the writer—ready to convey these feelings to an audience.

The foregoing advice is rather general; however, there are also specific things you can do to improve the tone of your story:

1. *Keep your characters consistent within themselves.* Make sure they behave and speak in accordance with their education, experience, cultural background, and temperament. Do you have a character who speaks in monosyllables and grunts in Chapter 1 and in long articulate sentences in Chapter 14?

2. *Keep your narrative consistent throughout the story.* Do you use flowery poetic constructions in one place and informal language or slang in others? A single ill-chosen word is enough to destroy the tone of a scene:

> Mrs. Feldman waddled into my office last Monday morning, and frankly, as soon as she told me what was on her mind, I figured she didn't have both oars in the water. I mean, why would her nephew tell her that he intended to poison her tapioca?
>
> "I'm sure he was joking, Mrs. Feldman," I said. "You admit he has no reason to kill you."
>
> "None that I know of," she said dolorously.

Dolorously? The word is obviously inappropriate. The narrator, who uses words such as *waddled* and *figured* and expressions such as *didn't have both oars in the water*, isn't going to describe Mrs. Feldman's speech as *dolorous*.

This kind of problem arises from careless use of a thesaurus. Synonyms are not interchangeable. They must be selected with an awareness of connotation and tone.

3. *Strive to keep the reader in a particular state of mind.* If you are writing an entertaining mystery, every page of it ought to entertain. You will handle the discovery of a murder, for example, in an entirely different way than if you were aiming to terrify your readers. If you want to entertain, you should play down the grisly details; if you want to terrify, play them up.

If you want to be entertaining, you shouldn't make the person who discovers the body too vulnerable and you will want to keep reader identification on the light side.

On the other hand, if you're aiming to terrify your readers, you should try to make the discoverer extremely vulnerable and attempt to get the readers to identify closely with him or her.

A strong and consistent tone in your writing is something that comes with practice. It is important because it not only helps to keep the readers in the imaginary world you have created, but it also works to provide that sense of unity that mystery fans like so much.

10
Technical Problems

Dialogue is a vital ingredient of fiction that serves several purposes. It helps to delineate your characters. What they say and how they say it reveals not only their opinions and attitudes, but it also shows a great deal about their personalities and their relationships to each other.

Dialogue provides information and so moves the story forward. It is helpful in arousing emotion in the readers, for dialogue provides a certain intimacy that narrative cannot. The readers are *seeing* and *hearing* the characters interacting.

Most important, however, dialogue is easy to read. Whereas many readers feel intimidated by a page full of narrative, they'll eagerly tackle a page of dialogue.

For all these reasons, it is good to use dialogue as much as possible in your story.

Handling Dialogue

Writing dialogue is often difficult for the beginner. Though you are striving for a semblance of reality in your conversations, you must avoid many things that actually do occur in real-life conversations. No one wants to read dialogue that is peppered with expressions like "you know" and "you see?" or the hesitation sounds "er" and "umm" and "uh."

And if you faithfully reproduce all the standard greetings and preliminary chit-chat that is part of normal conversation, your characters will spend a lot of time saying such things as, "Hello," "How are you?" "How's your Aunt Martha?" "Nice weather we're having, isn't it?" and other everyday trivia.

The principle to follow is: *Serve the meat only.* If it doesn't move the plot along or help to characterize the person speaking or help to establish the tone of the scene, omit it.

> After lunch I came upon Lucy sitting on the sun porch, polishing her nails a particularly violent shade of scarlet.
>
> "Did your mother ever tell you how she got the ivory madonna?" I asked.
>
> Lucy didn't bother looking up. "No. She never talked about it. Changed the subject whenever anyone mentioned it." She paused to blow on her nails and frowned. "But my cousin Ethel said something about it once—that some crimes deserve a special place in hell—and that was where my mother was going."
>
> "What did she mean by that?"
>
> Lucy shrugged. "I never found out. Mother walked into the room just then and threw an ashtray at her."
>
> A special place in hell? What had Lucy's mother done? Desecrated a church? Robbed a monastery? I figured it was time to have another talk with Brother Aloysius.

Notice that these characters neither greeted each other nor said good-bye. Readers assume that these things are done whenever appropriate. They also assume that more was said than was recorded. But the only thing the readers are interested in is that part of the conversation that is pertinent to the story.

Handling Attributives

A second common problem in writing dialogue is the handling of attributives—that is, those little phrases that attribute a line of dialogue to a character. The simplest attributives, of course, are *he said* and *she said*, and they ought to be used most of the time.

Sometimes beginners, alarmed at the number of *he saids* and *she saids* creeping into the manuscript, try to be creative with attributives. The result looks like this:

> "Aunt Martha's brooch isn't anywhere in the house," Brian stated flatly.

> "Maybe she put it into her safe deposit box," Connie suggested.

> "No," Brian replied. "I saw the record. She hasn't opened the box in months."

> "Whew!" Connie exclaimed. "Then we can be sure she hasn't changed her will again."

> "Why do you say that?" Brian questioned.

> "If she had, she'd have put a copy in the box," Connie answered.

> "Don't be too sure," Brian retorted. "You know how disorganized she is."

Tiresome, isn't it?

The important things to remember regarding attributives in conversation are:

1. The speaker need not be identified if it is clear—either from the content or the style of the speech—who is talking.

2. There is nothing wrong in using *he said* and *she said*. In fact, they ought to be the attributives of choice most of the time, because readers will slide over them easily, almost with-

out noticing. Other attributives, however, will be noticed and ought to be used sparingly. They are most effective when they serve a specific purpose, as for example:

> "Oh, no!" she cried. "That can't be!"
>
> "Why not?" he asked.
>
> "You damned bastard!" he shouted. "Get out of here!"

In each of these cases, the word *said* would have been inappropriate.

3. An action or a statement of fact may be used to attribute a line of dialogue to a character.

> "Where are you going?" Steve asked.
>
> Betsy pulled on her gloves. "Out."

Because Betsy's action is mentioned in the same paragraph as the response "Out," our readers will assume that Betsy was the person who spoke. We might as easily have stated a fact about Betsy:

> Betsy's face grew pale. "Out."

It is important to remember that whenever we use an action or a statement of fact to identify the speaker, a period—not a comma—should separate it from the line of dialogue.

> "It was a funny show," she said

But:

> "It was a funny show." She giggled.

Words can be spoken in many ways, but they cannot be giggled. Nor can they be laughed, smiled, chuckled, leered, snickered, frowned, or glowered. These are actions and must be treated as such grammatically.

FLASHBACKS

It is often necessary to give the readers some information regarding events in the past. If the information is brief, we can simply integrate it into the narrative in such a way that it establishes what has happened in the past without actually stopping the present action to return to the past.

> As Jessica drove over the crest of the hill, she caught sight of the cottage. It looked the same, she thought. After fifteen years, it hadn't changed much at all. The weathered shingles, the red shutters, the large window that faced the sea.
>
> The porch where she and Jed had played as children was sagging a little now. And the pier—how many times had Jed given her a brotherly shove into the water from that pier? It was missing a half dozen planks.
>
> Jessica pulled her car up alongside the cottage and set the parking brake.

Here we are giving the readers information about the past without actually going back and "seeing" past events happening. In this case, we want the readers to know that Jessica and her brother Jed had spent happy times at this cottage as children.

We could, of course, simply have put that information into straight narrative:

> She and Jed had had happy times at the cottage when they were children.

But, as you can see, that isn't as effective as presenting the images of the children playing on the porch and of Jed playfully pushing his sister into the water.

We have inserted this information about the past into the description of the porch and the pier as we are seeing them in the present. Thus, we haven't really stopped the action of our story, which is the main problem presented by a flashback.

Sometimes it *is* necessary to take the readers into the past and have them experience what happened:

> Jessica dug the bottle of Scotch out of her suitcase and found a glass in the kitchen cabinet. There was no ice, of course, and the tap water was warm, so she sipped the liquor straight. She looked at the door.
>
> Might as well get it over with, she thought. Waiting wasn't going to make it any easier. The screen door banged behind her as it had banged that morning so long ago.
>
> The sun had just been cracking the horizon and she had shivered in the morning air as she ran toward the water's edge.
>
> It was best to plunge right in, Jed always said. He was a great one for a quick swim at dawn. Of course, look who was sleeping late this morning! Probably had a hangover. It was a wonder that Dad hadn't caught on to Jed's sneaking out at night.
>
> Jessica slowed up as she reached the pier. A pile of rags had washed up beneath it. Her heart stopped. The blue plaid rag on top, rising and falling with each wave—Jed had a shirt like that—
>
> "Oh, God! Jed! Oh, dear God!"
>
> Dad heard her screams. He had told her later that he'd found her pulling Jed's body from the water. She'd never been able to remember that.

> Jessica removed her sandals as she came to the water's edge. She set them on the sand along with the now empty Scotch glass. Darkness was falling. The gulls were settling for the night. Beneath the pier the water was black.
>
> "Jed," she whispered, tears streaming down her cheeks as she walked into the water. "I'm coming."

In this case we have taken the readers into the past and let them experience Jessica's trauma at her brother's death. Even though we had to stop the action in the present for the moment, it was worth doing for two reasons: First, what happened during the flashback was dramatic. It adds to the suspense level of our story. If, on the other hand, we had flahsed back to show Jed and Jessica enjoying a beach party, it would have lessened the tension.

Second, knowing what Jessica experienced in the past helps our readers to understand her present state of mind. If Jessica's return to the cottage had nothing to do with her brother's death or if she weren't planning to commit suicide, there would be no reason to explore this unhappy memory of hers, no matter how dramatic it is.

Technically, a flashback is not difficult to execute. Notice that it begins and ends with a sentence or two in the past perfect tense:

> . . . as it *had* banged that morning. . . . The sun *had* just been cracking the horizon . . she *had* shivered . . .

and later:

> He *had* told later that *he'd* found. . . . *She'd* never been able to remember. . . .

Since we are telling our story in the simple past tense, when the readers come upon a sentence such as *She looked at the door*, they interpret that as happening in the present. Thus, it takes a past perfect tense to establish that certain events happened *prior* to the present time: She *had* shivered in the morning air.

To tell the whole flashback in the past perfect tense, however, would be tedious, and there is no need for it. After we have used the past perfect tense a couple of times, our readers will have oriented themselves and we can comfortably switch to the simple past tense. When we come to the end of the flashback, we again use the past perfect tense a couple of times to remind the readers that what we have been talking about happened prior to the present.

How many times do you need to use the past perfect tense before you can safely switch back to the simple past? As many times as is necessary to make the transition clear. Sometimes, once is enough. Often twice is plenty. In the foregoing example, it was necessary to put three verbs into the past perfect, for any fewer would have left some ambiguity in the reading.

One other point should be made. In the foregoing example, we used a simple device to help make the flashback seem to occur naturally. The banging of the screen door in the present reminds Jessica that the screen door also banged as she went out on the morning when she found Jed's body. The banging of the door serves to trigger her memory in the same way that our memory is often triggered in real life.

At the end of the flashback, we used another device to make sure that our readers know we are returning to the present. We show them the Scotch glass. Now it is clear that we are speaking about the adult Jessica again.

Flashbacks can be an effective way to introduce material from the past into your story, but they should not be used indiscriminately. The longer the flashback, the greater the risk of destroying the momentum of your story.

Before using a flashback, ask yourself whether it is the

most effective way to convey the material at hand to the readers. If it will add to the drama and suspense of your story, go ahead and use it. If it tends to lower the suspense level, look for another method of introducing the material.

HANDLING TENSES EFFECTIVELY

As we mentioned in the previous section, most stories are told in the simple past tense and readers interpret it as if they were seeing the events happening. Thus, in order to make the readers see Millie sitting down at the table, we say:

> Millie sat down at the table.

And in order to describe events that happened earlier, we use the past perfect tense. Thus, if we want the readers to know that Millie witnessed a bank robbery before she came to the table, we say:

> Millie had witnessed a bank robbery that morning.

Now, suppose we want to tell the readers something that Millie is planning to do in the future. We simply use a past form of the future tense:

> She would order a martini. Maybe a double. That would calm her nerves.

Keeping your tenses consistent is an effective way to help your readers stay in your imaginary world. If you use tenses correctly, your readers will scarcely be aware of them. But the incorrect use of tenses can severely damage your story by confusing your readers.

One further point ought to be made. Beware of using

the present tense in your narrative when the story is being told in the simple past. This is sometimes done intentionally to evoke a storytelling manner:

> On Saturday afternoon, Scamp curled up beside me on the sofa as he often does when I read.

There is nothing grammatically wrong with this, but look what happens. By the use of the present tense in the word *does*, the readers are being made aware that it is not Saturday now. It is a just a bit harder to see Scamp curling up on the sofa because he isn't doing it *now*. The feeling of *being told* about past events instead of *being shown* present ones has crept into that sentence.

The whole problem can be avoided by sticking to the simple past tense:

> On Saturday afternoon, Scamp curled up beside me on the sofa as he often did when I was reading.

Now our readers can comfortably imagine that it is Saturday and that they are *seeing* Scamp curl up on the sofa.

A subtle point, perhaps, but one worth noting.

11

Maintaining Suspense

Suspense! That is the stuff of which mysteries are made. As an author, one of your chief goals is to keep your readers turning pages, to fill them with an intense desire to find out what happens next. What causes that desire? Suspense, of course!

WHAT IS SUSPENSE?

Suspense is *anxiety* created by *uncertainty*. There are other definitions, but this one is particularly enlightening to the writer. Consider: You must make your readers *anxious* and *keep* them that way until you have finished telling your story.

How Suspense Is Created

When do you become anxious? Not all uncertainty produces anxiety. Suppose it looks as though it might rain tomorrow. There's doubt. Is there anxiety? Not if you're planning on staying home and baking bread!

What if you've planned to attend the company picnic? Now will the threat of rain make you anxious? Not likely. But what if your only daughter is getting married in the morning and you've planned a garden ceremony and two hundred guests are coming—far more than you can accommodate in your home? Now you ought to be getting anxious—not only because a wedding is more important than a picnic and cannot as easily be rescheduled but because it's *your* daughter's wedding. The personal element makes a big difference!

One further example: Suppose it has been raining steadily for several days. You are standing on a hill overlooking the town and you see that the reservoir is filled to the brim and the dam, which overlooks a valley full of homes, is threatening to burst under the unaccustomed pressure. Small cracks are already forming.

In this situation, the possibility of more rain in the morning takes on ominous proportions. Much more than a picnic or a ceremony is at stake. Homes and lives may be lost. Are you feeling anxiety? Of course! And you'll feel even more if one of those homes is yours, and more yet if your family is in it!

The principles are becoming clear: *The more that hangs in the balance, the greater the suspense in waiting for the outcome.* Also: *Suspense is increased when the stakes are personal.*

There's an important corollary to that last statement. It *is* possible to have suspense even when there are no personal stakes involved. Dramatic circumstances alone can sometimes be enough to create suspense, but it will be shorter lived.

Let's go back to that dam that is nearly bursting. If you were standing on that hill watching, you'd feel a certain amount of anxiety for the people below even if you had never met any of them. Such empathetic emotion is what impels a stranger to rush into a burning house to save a child. You must remember, however, that there is a limit to the amount of empathy one feels toward a stranger. How many stories have you read in the papers telling of people standing by while someone was robbed, beaten, raped, or murdered?

It is best, then, not to depend upon circumstances alone to create suspense for any but the briefest periods. Whenever possible, give the readers a personal stake in the outcome. Make them *care* what happens.

To illustrate how this can be done, let's begin putting a plot together.

Let's make the crime a murder that our hero is going to solve. We might make the circumstances a little bizarre in order to arouse our readers' curiosity. Suppose that Mr. Gruen, a banker, lights his pipe before going to bed one night and he drops dead because the stem of his pipe was coated with a cyanide solution. Our hero—we'll make him a likable private eye named Jared Ball—is called into the case by the dead man's daughter, Cynthia, who is accused of the murder.

Have we produced suspense? Not really. What happens if Jared doesn't solve the case? A woman will go to jail—a woman he doesn't really know. A woman, perhaps, that he doesn't even like.

How can we inject suspense into the situation? One obvious method is to make Jared care about the girl—the more, the better. In fact, let's say they're engaged to be married.

This is no longer a routine case. Jared will be anxious to remove suspicion from his fiancée. And if we make Jared a character with whom the readers can identify, they'll be anxious, too.

And now that we have a suspenseful idea to work with, let's find a good beginning for this story.

SUSPENSEFUL BEGINNINGS

Inexperienced writers too often set out to tell a story in an exact chronology and it is often a mistake. Serious crimes and deep personal and interpersonal conflicts do not just happen. They come about only after a long sequence of events that shaped the characters involved.

A murder, for example, may be the culmination of a series of personal conflicts that began when the murderer and victim were children. But to start telling the story with the minor conflicts of childhood would result in a very slow opening. In these days of television and movies, audiences are accustomed to *action*. They expect things to begin happening immediately.

If someone picks up a book, he's pretty sure to look at the first few paragraphs and probably will read a couple of pages. But if the author hasn't caught his attention by then, he may go no farther.

Accordingly, we must place inordinate value on the first few pages of our book, and the first couple of paragraphs should be priceless. This is our chance—and it may be our only chance—to hook the readers, to catch their attention and hold it so firmly that they cannot *possibly* stop reading.

A good rule is to *begin your story when something important is happening, has just happened, or is about to happen.* How do you decide? Sometimes you have the option and sometimes the decision is made for you.

Suppose, for example, that we want to begin our book with the murder of Mr. Gruen. If we are telling the story from Jared's point of view exclusively, we can't show the readers the death scene unless Jared was there at the time. Let's say he was not.

We still have the choice of beginning the story just before the murder—perhaps Jared had dinner with Cynthia's family that evening—or just after—when Jared first learns about it.

Which would be better? It will depend. We ought to be able to find plenty of suspense in having Jared learn that his future father-in-law has been murdered and that his fiancée is accused of having done it.

Could there be suspense in the dinner scene as well? It depends on what happened at that dinner. If it was a congenial meal with no particular conflicts or tensions, it doesn't belong at the beginning of our book.

But suppose it was a troubled repast. Cynthia's father voiced disapproval of her upcoming marriage. Perhaps he threatened to disinherit her if she chose to marry someone as socially undesirable as a private eye.

And how did Cynthia react? Did she burst into tears? Did she get angry and even threaten her father? Or did she take his disapproval quite calmly?

Which is best? The answer is obviously not clear-cut, for all three reactions can cast suspicion on Cynthia in retrospect. But there's a lot to be said for unpredictable turns in a story. The element of surprise is one of the delights of a satisfying plot.

So let's say that Cynthia didn't get upset when her father threatened to cut her out of his will. That accomplishes a good purpose: Our readers will have to wonder why she isn't distressed, and after Mr. Gruen has been killed, they'll have to suspect Cynthia. (Could it be that she knew even then that her father would never have a chance to change his will?)

Of course, we will have a logical reason why she acted in this way—a reason that is consistent with her innocence. And we'll explain that to the readers at the proper time.

Now, however, though we've done something positive by having Cynthia behave in an unexpected way, we have created more work for ourselves. Her calm reaction has drained all of the tension from the dinner scene.

What can we do? We can create tension by having other things happen. Mr. Gruen might quarrel with Cynthia's brother, Harold, over Harold's mismanagement of bank investments. We can show that Harold resents working for his father. We might also see an obvious coolness between Mr. Gruen and his wife, Lucille.

These sources of tension in our opening scene should provide possible motives for the murder. In this case, Harold and Mrs. Gruen will also be suspected of the murder at certain points in the story.

How will we know if we have enough tension in the dinner scene to make it a good beginning? It's a judgment call, really. We may have to write the scene before we can decide whether or not we want to keep it as our opening.

KEEPING UP THE CONFLICT

Any time suspicion falls upon Cynthia, Jared experiences conflict. He loves her. He believes she's innocent—at least he *wants* to believe she's innocent. But how much evidence can he explain away?

Conflict is one of the chief sources of anxiety. Generally, it is also what keeps your story moving, because when people experience anxiety, they react by doing something to reduce it.

Thus, logically Jared knows that Cynthia looks guilty. Emotionally, however, he cannot accept her guilt. He must do something to resolve the conflict he feels. He *must* search for the truth.

And though this conflict is something Jared experiences from within, we also can create conflict between Jared and Cynthia. Suppose she refuses to answer his questions? Suppose she tells him something that is obviously untrue? As long as Cynthia is less than candid with Jared, there will be tension between them. Since our readers care about Cynthia and Jared, they'll experience that tension, too.

There's a lesser kind of tension we can use in our story as well. Imagine that you are sitting in a restaurant and two people at the next table begin quarreling. They are not creating an obvious scene; their voices are just loud enough for you to overhear.

Even if you don't know these two people, you'll feel uncomfortable. Your tension level has gone up simply by witnessing conflict. Thus, if we can logically put even two minor characters at odds with each other, it can raise the level of tension in our story.

ADDING COMPLICATIONS

Complications are necessary in a story of any length because of a basic psychological principle: Human beings are extremely adaptable. Given time, they will adjust to living even under the worst of conditions. What may cause terrific anxiety in Chapter 1 will be a nagging worry by Chapter 3 and only an ordinary problem by Chapter 8 *unless the situation has worsened in the meantime.*

Let's go back to our story. From the first, the police are inclined to suspect Cynthia because she stood to lose a large inheritance if her father lived long enough to change his will. Her brother is a lesser suspect because he and Mr. Gruen had quarreled. But Mr. Gruen did not threaten Harold.

Now, how do we create complications to make things look worse for Cynthia? Suppose Jared finds out she bought the cyanide? And even better than that, suppose she lied about it?

How much suspense can we get out of that? It will depend upon the way we handle the material.

We could write about these events in a straightforward manner. Cynthia is asked directly—by the police or by Jared—whether she knows where the cyanide came from. Nervously, she says no. A short time later, as the police are checking drugstores in the city, a pharmacist identifies

Cynthia as the person who purchased sodium cyanide from him a few days earlier. Although she signed a false name to the poison control register, the handwriting is unquestionably Cynthia's.

What has happened? Although Cynthia lied, it didn't take the readers long to find that out. In short order they have become certain of the truth. Is there a better way to handle the same material? Could we have gotten more suspense out of it?

MILKING A SITUATION
FOR SUSPENSE

Let's go back and rewrite these same events in a less straightforward manner, remembering that we are seeking to create anxiety generated by *uncertainty*.

Suppose Jared learns that the police have found a pharmacist who says he recently sold some sodium cyanide to an attractive young woman. Our readers' hearts should beat a little faster at this, for Cynthia is the only attractive young woman in the story so far.

Our hero feels compelled to check this information out and goes to see the pharmacist. He tells Jared that the woman in question gave him the name Audrey Grafer and that she had long dark hair. This last bit of information is a relief to Jared, for Cynthia is a blonde.

See what we've done? For a few minutes we pointed the finger of suspicion at Cynthia, then turned it away. At the same time, we've raised new questions: Who is Audrey Grafer, and did she have anything to do with Mr. Gruen's death?

A good rule to remember is: *Whenever you answer a question even partially (thus reducing tension), be sure to raise another question (which will elevate tension again).*

Have we made Audrey Grafer important enough to draw suspicion away from Cynthia? After all, at this point she's little more than a name. What else can the pharmacist tell us about her?

Suppose he joked with her about buying such a lethal substance. She must have given him a reasonable explanation.

The pharmacist tells Jared that Audrey said she was a laboratory assistant to Herman Jenkins, a professor of physics at the local college. Professor Jenkins had broken his only bottle of sodium cyanide that morning and needed some more for an electroplating demonstration that he was going to present to his afternoon class. As the chemical supply house was some distance away, he'd sent Audrey to see whether she could get some from a local pharmacy in time for the class.

Now Audrey Grafer is more than just a name. The readers should have a mental image of an educated, intelligent, and resourceful young woman. But again, in answering the question of why Audrey wanted the cyanide, we've lowered the suspense level and we need to raise another question. Something must be amiss.

Suppose the pharmacist remarks that he wondered why a woman would wear such expensive clothes if she were working in a laboratory where she was handling chemicals. She had said she'd just come from the lab and that she was hurrying back to make the class—and yet she was wearing a cashmere sweater and calfskin shoes.

Expensive clothes speak of wealth. Even if we say nothing directly, the readers will think of Cynthia. They should be uncertain again.

As the story moves on, we'll uncover more information incriminating to Cynthia. Perhaps our hero sees her trying to hide a dark wig. Suspicious. But Cynthia explains—rather convincingly—that she bought it long ago to wear to a masquerade party and now she's afraid that if the police discover she owns such a wig, they'd accuse her of having posed as Audrey. Since she's been so reticent before this, her seeming candor leaves Jared at a loss.

Then the police announce that their handwriting expert says there is a high degree of likelihood that the signature on the poison control record was written by Cynthia. (Note that he is not absolutely certain!)

And as we discover details like this that point to Cynthia's guilt, we'll also acquire information that points away from it, just to keep the readers off balance.

Eventually it will become clear that Cynthia did indeed disguise herself as Audrey, buy the cyanide, and lie about it afterward, but we'll have gotten a lot of suspense out of that question in the meantime. And of course, by now we'll have made sure that the readers realize that just because Cynthia bought the poison, it doesn't mean she is the one who used it. To make matters even less clear, Cynthia won't explain *why* she did these things—at least not for a few more chapters. We may as well get as much suspense out of that question as we can!

Directing Suspicion Elsewhere

Even though Cynthia may look very guilty at a given moment, we can still make the readers feel uncertain about her guilt by directing suspicion elsewhere.

Who else can we point a finger at? Cynthia's brother, Harold? Their mother, Lucille? How about someone outside the family—say, Mr. Gruen's business partner, Sam Blue? As long as we can give each of them a logical motive for committing murder and the opportunity to have done so, they can all be good suspects.

Let's look at Harold and decide what he's been up to. We know Mr. Gruen was angry with him, that something was amiss with the bank's investments. Has Harold mismanaged the money through stupidity or malice?

What kind of a person is Harold? For purposes of the plot, it would be good if Cynthia cares a lot about him. Then the readers will be uncomfortable whenever suspicion is directed toward Harold. If he's Cynthia's older brother, he's likely to have been protective of her, and she's likely to admire him. If he's her younger brother, she'll probably have maternal feelings toward him. She'll excuse his weaknesses and try to protect him from problems of his own making.

Whatever we decide, Harold will have to have an appealing side to his character. Otherwise, the readers won't understand why Cynthia cares about him. The fact that he is her brother is not enough. Too many brothers and sisters hate each other.

Now we have to figure out what Harold has done and how it fits into our story. Perhaps Cynthia won't tell Jared why she bought the cyanide because she's protecting Harold. Then it would make sense for him to be the younger of the two and to have a prominent weakness—say, gambling.

What if Harold asked Cynthia to help him win a wager? What if one of his acquaintances had bet a great deal of money that Harold couldn't obtain a highly poisonous substance from legitimate sources right in the city without the friend being able to find out how he did it.

In retrospect, of course, the setup seems highly suspect, but at the time Harold proposed the idea to his sister, there seemed no harm in it—and he *really* needed the money! Of course, he didn't happen to mention to Cynthia who his friend was.

What happens next? After the murder, both Harold and Cynthia are thrown into a state of conflict. They fear for themselves and for each other. And Cynthia may not be completely sure of Harold's innocence.

Since we're writing from Jared's point of view, we will

see only the tangible results of these conflicts. Cynthia and Harold will be nervous, evasive, and perhaps unusually cool toward each other. Such uncharacteristic behavior ought to raise a lot of questions in the minds of the readers.

USING SUBPLOTS
TO GENERATE SUSPENSE

As we mentioned in Chapter 3, every important character in a story can carry off a subplot. A mystery novel is a lot like macrame. Several strands (story lines) are woven neatly together into a single entity. At times the strands are knotted so that at certain points we cannot be sure which strand we are looking at.

By generating a couple of subplots, we'll find it much easier to keep up the suspense in our story. Whenever things are slowing down in the particular story line we're following, we can pull up another strand for examination. We can always find someone who's getting into deeper trouble.

How do we generate these subplots? Remember what we said earlier? Give each character a personal problem to wrestle with. In this case, Harold has an addiction to gambling—and look where it's got him!

It isn't hard to work the subplots together, either. Just consider how one character's failings will affect another character. Look at Lucille Gruen. She and her husband must have quarreled before his last dinner. Over what? Cynthia's engagement? Harold's gambling? His mishandling of the bank investments?

Perhaps Mrs. Gruen has been having an affair. What brought that on? Hasn't Mr. Gruen been paying her enough attention? Why not? Has he been too wrapped up in his work? Was that *his* problem? If so, how did that affect his partner, Sam?

Once you start asking questions and answering them, the story begs to be written. The subplots will come easily enough if you turn your attention from one character to another as you ask the questions.

BUILDING SUSPENSE
WITH DRAMATIC EVENTS

In each story line there are going to be possibilities for drama. Consider Harold. If he isn't the murderer, perhaps the person with whom he made the bet *is*, and *he* now wishes to seal Harold's lips forever. Somewhere in the book, then, we could have Harold murdered or have an attempt made on his life.

As we said earlier, it is often good technique to use such an event to reverse the story line. Suppose we're in the middle of Chapter 10 and we've piled up as much evidence and suspicion against Harold as we can logically do. The readers are pretty certain that he must be the murderer. Then someone puts a bullet into Harold's brain. All that certainty is suddenly gone, and we're off and running again.

One point needs to be made here. We could also suppose that the murderer of Mr. Gruen is *not* the person with whom Harold made the bet, but someone else who took advantage of the cyanide being in the house. We could still have an attempt on Harold's life, *provided it comes about as a logical consequence of his behavior.*

For example, because he's a gambler, he might owe someone a lot of money that he can't repay. That someone might choose to exact a different kind if payment.

Of course, we're not going to create this murder attempt out of a void. We'll have clearly established earlier that Harold is in financial trouble, and that he owes money to some unsavory characters who play rough when they don't get their money. And the nice thing is that, as we establish these things, they'll tend to make Harold look guilty. A young man in his position might be desperate enough to do anything to get the money he needs—even murder his father for an inheritance.

Then, with the crack of a bullet, Harold is no longer a likely suspect. Now he's another victim. And the same facts which made Harold look possibly guilty of murdering his father now work to make him a believable victim.

THE USE AND ABUSE
OF RED HERRINGS

A good deal of suspense can be maintained by the proper use of a red herring. A red herring is nothing more than a distraction. The term comes from the hunting practice of pulling a herring across the path to draw off the hounds. That is exactly what we want to do with the readers from time to time.

When do you use a red herring? Suppose logic demands that a question be asked at a particular time and there is no logical reason why it shouldn't be answered just then. If, for purposes of either maintaining suspense or protecting the solution of the plot, you feel that your readers must not have that information just yet, a red herring is in order.

As an example, let's imagine a scene between Cynthia and Jared in the drawing room of the Gruen mansion. Jared has just come from the bank, where one of the officers mentioned that Mr. Gruen occasionally took important papers home so that he could work on them at night. Jared asks Cynthia where her father would put such documents until he could take them back to the bank. Cynthia tells him that there is a wall safe in the library. It is only logical that Jared ask her whether or not she knows the combination. And, according to our plot, she *must* know it.

Now suppose that we know that once Jared sees what is in the safe, it won't be long before the murderer is revealed and we still have a couple of things that must happen before then. What do we do? Why, the door to the drawing room bursts open and a distraught Mrs. Gruen announces that the hospital has just called. Harold (who was shot a couple of chapters earlier and has been lingering in a coma ever since) is near death.

Jared and Cynthia have no choice. Looking in the safe will have to wait. They rush off to the hospital.

You must remember, however that *the readers must always feel that Jared and Cynthia are behaving logically under the circumstances.*

Suppose, for example, Cynthia had said, "Sure, I know the combination, but let's wait until after dinner to open the safe. Otherwise I won't have time to fix my hair." The readers would be terribly dissatisfied. This is too obviously an attempt to keep information from them.

A red herring may be an interruption, as we've just seen. It may also be the discovery of an object or a piece of information, the true significance of which is not apparent.

Let's imagine that Jared comes upon Mrs. Gruen burning some letters in the fireplace. The act itself tends to make our readers suspicious of Mrs. Gruen. Furthermore, she appears to be nervous when she realizes that Jared has seen her. And she won't tell him what she was burning. Now the readers should be wondering whether Mrs. Gruen could be the killer.

Later we'll show that the letters were from Mrs. Gruen's lover and she was afraid that the police would discover them and a scandal would ensue. Although she was not the murderer, her behavior was both logical and relevant to the story (provided, of course, that we have established her as a person who would abhor a scandal and at least hinted that she has a lover).

One thing we are *never* allowed to do is to plant false or irrelevant clues to distract our readers. The difference is that a false clue is illogical while an irrelevant one may be logical, but it simply doesn't belong in the story.

To illustrate, suppose we go back to the scene where Jared finds Mrs. Gruen burning some letters. She gets flustered and refuses to explain what she is doing. Later, the readers are told that Mrs. Gruen finds it therapeutic to do cleaning whenever she is upset and that she was simply cleaning out her desk. There was no importance whatsoever in the letters that she burned. This is a *false* clue. There was no reason for Mrs. Gruen to get flustered or to refuse to explain her actions. Her behavior was *illogical*.

On the other hand, suppose that instead of getting flustered, she calmly explains that she is only cleaning out her desk as a therapeutic release. If there is no importance in her actions or in the letters, this incident is irrelevant to the story and it is unfair to arouse the readers' suspicions on an irrelevant point.

However, suppose Mrs. Gruen calmly explains that she is cleaning out her desk as a way to relieve tension and Jared accepts her explanation at face value. Then, later in the story it is discovered that a letter of some importance is missing. Now the letter-burning incident assumes significance. Did Mrs. Gruen destroy the letter Jared is looking for, or didn't she?

This will be a nice red herring if it turns out that she did *not* burn the letter. It is a lovely legitimate clue if she *did*.

THE CLIMAX

The climax of our story should be that moment at which the level of suspense—reader anxiety—is the greatest. Never have things looked so dark for our hero. Everything that can possibly go wrong has done so.

The climax should come as near the end of our story as possible. The problems in creating a successful climax are essentially:

1. Making sure that suspense builds steadily up to the climax.
2. Making the climax as suspenseful as possible.
3. Quickly resolving the anxieties of a suspenseful climax into a satisfying ending.

As you might imagine, this requires a bit of planning and depends a good deal on structuring your story properly. In Chapter 12 we'll discuss structure.

12

Structure

The structure of a story is like the framework of a house. It is not apparent when you are looking at the finished product, but it is what holds the thing together and gives it a shape. A well-structured story gives the readers a sense of order and unity.

Structure is what makes the readers feel that they should have seen the solution earlier.

A good structure can also provide a lot of the suspense in your story. It can make your readers say afterward, "I couldn't put that book down!"

How do you go about structuring a mystery story? Since there is no one right way to put a story together, it is impossible to set out step-by-step rules to follow in this matter. However, it is helpful to consider a few elements that are necessary to a good mystery story and see whether or not your structure will provide them.

THE QUALITIES OF GOOD STRUCTURE

1. *Does your story hook your readers from the beginning?* A good beginning will draw your readers into your story, making them so interested that they want desperately to find out

what happens next. Does your story have a gripping beginning or does it start out slowly—too slowly? Sometimes rearranging the structure can solve the problem of a beginning that doesn't hook the readers.

Suppose, for example, that we are writing a story about Laurie, a young commercial artist who is being stalked by a psychopathic killer. If the story is being told chronologically from Laurie's point of view, she probably won't be aware for some time that she's being watched. And if she isn't aware, obviously she—and the readers—will feel no anxiety, so there's no point in telling this part of the story.

But suppose, because of the way our plot is constructed, something important *does* happen during this time. The thing is, its importance isn't going to be apparent until later.

We may need to change the structure of our story. We could start out with a prologue, told from the point of view of the killer, showing him selecting Laurie as his next victim. Then, when the story proper begins, we can switch to Laurie's point of view and stay there. Even if she is feeling no anxiety, the readers will be. They know what's going on, even if she doesn't.

Another option would be to begin our story at or near the point when Laurie becomes aware of possible danger. Then we will have to flash back for any necessary material.

Whichever way the story is written, our readers should have a good idea early in the story what the main problem is going to be.

2. *Have the protagonist and the villain both been introduced early in the story?* The reason for introducing the protagonist early should be obvious by now—we want to establish strong reader identification as soon as possible. But it's easy to forget the importance of introducing the villain early and keeping him or her in front of the reader. This principle is especially important in the writing of a whodunit, where the identity of the villain is not revealed until the very end.

Remember what we said in Chapter 5? *The reader is most satisfied when the villain turns out to be a familiar character.* This is because the shock value of the revelation depends upon how unexpected it is. The more our readers feel that they know a given character well, the more unexpected will be the revelation that he or she is the villain.

Here is a problem: How do we make the readers feel they know the villain well without giving away that character's villainous nature? One thing we can do is get the villain onstage early and keep him or her there as much as possible during the story. And our readers should see the villain *in action*, not merely being part of the background.

How can we accomplish this? Remember that the villain is a person with an occupation and relationships with other people. The villain is somebody's parent or sibling or spouse, somebody's friend or neighbor or business partner or client.

Suppose, for example, that our villain, Horace, is a concert violinist. We've gotten right into the problem and had the murder committed early. The concertmaster has had his head bashed in.

Our protagonist is going to be Police Inspector Pullman, who is called to the scene of the murder. However, we have no logical reason for Inspector Pullman to consider Horace a suspect until after the inspector has gotten certain information from three other characters. It looks like it will be a while before Horace gets onstage. How can we get him there sooner?

First, we can ask ourselves how is Horace related to the three other characters who will appear earlier? We have Walter, a fellow violinist, Ethel, who plays first flute, and Lisa, the concertmaster's sister.

Walter could live in the same apartment building as Horace. That way, if the inspector visits Walter to question him, Horace could logically drop in to borrow a piece of rosin or to return the eggs he borrowed yesterday.

Or Ethel could have a young son who takes violin lessons from Horace. And when the inspector comes to see Ethel, Horace could be there, giving the boy a lesson.

Or perhaps Lisa has designs on Horace. Faced with the tragic death of her brother, she turns to Horace for sympathy. Again, Horace would logically be around.

Such added relationships often generate small subplots that must be woven into our story. Sometimes, they necessitate changing the order of events. The story structure may need to be considerably altered to accommodate them. The inconvenience, however, is worth the effort if we succeed in keeping our villain onstage.

One other point ought to be made here. The villain cannot be put onstage solely for the purpose of having him or her in front of the audience. Any character who appears in a scene—whether in the theater or in fiction—must further the story. He or she must do or say something that conveys information vital to the plot or that develops a character or a relationship.

3. *If there is more than one point of view in your story, is there a good balance or a pattern in the changing views?* It is especially important to consider the structure of your story when you use more than one viewpoint in it. Although changing viewpoint tends to lower reader identification, by organizing your material well you can provide your readers with other satisfactions: the sense of unity and the sense of order.

There are any number of ways to organize your material. If, for example, you have two characters of equal importance, you might like to alternate viewpoint from chapter to chapter. Another possibility would be to tell the first third or so of the book from the viewpoint of one character, the middle third from the viewpoint of a second character, and return to the first viewpoint for the remainder of the book.

It isn't necessary to have a completely rigid or absolutely symmetrical structure, of course. But be aware that both pattern and balance in your structure give your readers satisfaction. Watch out when your structure becomes disorganized or unbalanced. If your first fifteen chapters are told from one viewpoint and the next one from a second viewpoint, three more from a third, and the last from the second again, your readers will probably feel they have been abandoned.

This doesn't mean that you can't have a number of viewpoints in your story. It only means that you need to take a lot of care with your structure. Sometimes it helps to think of the various viewpoints as colored blocks. If the first chapter is from the view of Andrew, the protagonist, picture a red block. If the second chapter is in Emma's view, there's a blue block and so forth. You should, of course, have more red blocks than any other color, for the protagonist has to be onstage most of the time. You also need to have red blocks occurring at regular intervals. Your readers will feel that you are forgetting something if you write six chapters in a row without coming back to Andrew's view.

The other colors ought to be distributed in a pleasing manner. Not all at one end or at the other. By experimenting you can discover the most effective way to balance the various views.

It is good to remember that the colored-block method is simplistic and cannot be followed blindly. For example, you might not ordinarily want to write four chapters in a row from Emma's viewpoint, for it might seem that your balance is being thrown off. But suppose that during two of those chapters Emma is watching Andrew. Even though the readers don't know what is going on in the protagonist's mind, he is still very much onstage. Are those two blocks red or blue or a little of both? You have to use your instincts to decide where the best balance is in such cases.

4. *Does tension mount steadily?* It is a beginner's mistake to have a gruesome murder with all the gory details right in the beginning and then follow with seventeen chapters of con-

versations, speculations, deductions, and inferences until someone finally comes up with the solution.

Remember what we said in Chapter 11? Suspense is *anxiety*. Mystery readers want to feel that danger is lurking around every corner. They want to feel *scared!* And they want to be more anxious with every chapter. This means that you have to arrange your story so that the situation keeps getting worse, that it produces more anxiety as time passes.

But it is another beginner's mistake to simply kill someone else off whenever the tension level starts falling. After a few such gratuitous slayings, even murder becomes boring.

In Chapter 11 we also said that most tension arises from conflict and that such conflict can either be within a character or between two or more characters. Accordingly, check your story structure not only for those events that raise the anxiety level of your readers but also for conflict within and among the characters.

For example, suppose Penny and Roberta were schoolmates. After a separation of twelve years, they meet, discover they are each planning a vacation in the Caribbean, and decide to go together. When they check into the villa they've rented, they discover a pool of blood on the kitchen floor. Surprisingly, the police don't seem to think it's important. "Now if you found a *body*," they say, "that would be different."

Penny, the protagonist, wants to leave. She feels she cannot enjoy her vacation here. Roberta wants to stay. She is reassuring and protective. And, after all, it *is* the height of the tourist season. They are not likely to find other accommodations. Penny decides that her friend is right.

Look at the tension level in this story. Finding a pool of blood in one's kitchen is an anxiety-raising event, yes. But what happens after that tends to lower tension levels. The police aren't upset. Roberta isn't upset. In fact, she's reassuring. In the end, Penny no longer feels she has to leave the villa.

How can we change things so that tension is building here? Well, suppose that the police aren't so offhand about that blood. Suppose they are surly and closemouthed, asking a lot of questions and not answering any. Now Penny—and the readers—will feel that something important is going on—but what?

And then, instead of having Roberta be a supportive, protective person, let's make her become either withdrawn and secretive or terrified and dependent upon Penny for emotional support.

Either way, Penny will feel she's on her own. She must make the decisions and no one is going to help her. Now if circumstances conspire to keep the two women at the villa, the tension level should be considerably higher than before.

How will this affect the structure of the story? It depends upon where the story is going, of course. Let's suppose that the two women have stumbled upon the scene of a murder. The killer got the body away before the women arrived, but he didn't have time to clean up the scene or to remove a damaging bit of evidence—evidence that Penny discovers without realizing its significance. Thus, we have set things up so the killer will be after Penny to protect himself.

If we make Roberta a frightened and dependent type, we probably won't have to change much, except those parts where she acts on her own initiative.

If, however, we have her become withdrawn, we'll need to generate a subplot to explain her behavior. Perhaps she has a secret in her past—something that has created an enemy. Now she thinks that her enemy is here to even the score. This may require a considerable change in the structure of the story that we originally planned, but it is the better option, for now Penny and Roberta can be in conflict much of the time.

Whenever Roberta turns silent, tells an obvious lie, or goes off by herself for a while, Penny—and the readers—will have to wonder how much Roberta can be trusted.

It seems a strange—and heartless—rule: *In order to keep tension up, keep your characters unhappy, worried, frightened, or in conflict until the end of the story, when they resolve their problems.* 5. *Does the climax come as near the end of the story as possible?* You may need to change the structure of your story if you find that you have a good deal of unfinished business to take care of after that scene in which excitement is at a peak—no more than a couple of paragraphs for a short story, no more than a few pages for a novel.

If you have a lot of material following the climax, consider how you might rearrange it so that most of it is taken care of before the climax. Can you wind up a subplot earlier? Can you answer many of the questions earlier, so that a sentence or two after the climax resolves a subplot, for example?

Let's suppose that little Kristin Hapwell, the two-year-old daughter of a well-known oil magnate, has been kidnapped and a demand of five million dollars ransom has been made. The authorities have learned the identity of one of the kidnappers and he is particularly violent and unfeeling. Throughout the book, the readers don't know whether or not Kristin is still alive. And because she suffers from diabetes and has been without medication, they can't be sure she'll be all right even if she is alive.

James and Sarah, Kristin's parents, have been having marital problems for some time and are now at odds over the way the investigation is being handled. It looks as though there is no hope for their marriage.

Since Kristin's parents are well known, her picture has often been in the papers and in magazines. In real life, it might happen that Kristin is recognized by a total stranger as the kidnappers move from one hideout to another. Suspicious, the stranger calls the police, who rescue the child. In the process, one of the kidnappers gets away. The little girl is in a diabetic coma and a deteriorated physical condition. It takes a week or so before doctors can reassure the parents that she'll make a complete recovery. A month later, the escaped kidnapper is picked up in another state when he tries to hold up a liquor store. Kristin's parents, drawn together during the week the child's recovery was uncertain, reconcile.

Even though things do happen that way in real life, it doesn't make good fiction. Look at the level of tension during these events. If the story is told from the parents' point of view, they will experience a great sense of relief when they learn that their daughter is alive. But there is still the uncertainty of possible physical damage as a result of her trauma. So the level of tension is lowered but not eliminated.

The fact that one of the kidnappers has escaped is not a source of anxiety, for he no longer poses a threat to them. However, the fact that he got away temporarily dilutes the feeling of satisfaction that might have been experienced had he been caught immediately. Furthermore, the amount of time that passes before it is known that Kristin will be all right and that her parents will reconcile makes both those revelations less dramatic.

Drama is also missing from both the discovery of Kristin's whereabouts and the capture of the last kidnapper, for they are accomplished by characters of lesser importance or characters offstage—people we don't know.

The result of all this is that tension levels recede gradually. It would be far more effective if we could restructure the ending so that each problem comes to a crisis at the same time and everything gets resolved as quickly as possible. Furthermore, if the story is being told from the point of view of James or Sarah or both, we want to have both of them involved in events at the climax.

Since the police know the identity of one of the kidnappers, they would have a picture of him and thus James and Sarah would recognize him if they saw him.

Suppose they do? Suppose they stop at a corner grocery to get some cigarettes and they see the man coming out. He's carrying a bag of groceries and right on top is a box of a popular sugar-filled cereal.

There is no time to call the police. James and Sarah follow the man's car, agonizing over Kristin's possible condition if the kidnappers are feeding her sugary foods. Each comes to realize that what is most important to both of them is that their daughter is all right. Previous problems seem insignificant. The readers sense that if Kristin is rescued, James and Sarah are likely to get back together.

See what is happening? While we are heightening the tension over Kristin's condition, we're beginning to resolve one of the subplots—James's and Sarah's relationship. We haven't totally resolved that problem—nobody's making any promises at this time—but we've gotten them to the point where things can be settled quickly.

They follow the man to a motel. Sarah slips away to call the police while James watches to make sure they don't get away. Suddenly the door to the motel room opens and two men and a woman come out. One of the men is carrying two suitcases. The woman has a large basket of laundry.

James realizes that they are changing hideouts. He must not let them get away before the police arrive. He pulls his car behind theirs, cutting off their escape. Sarah returns to see James confront the two men. One of the kidnappers pulls a gun and wounds James as the police arrive. The kidnappers are quickly taken into custody. James, clutching his wounded shoulder, charges into the motel room and finds it empty.

It is Sarah who spots the laundry basket in the backseat of the kidnappers' car. Beneath some dirty clothing is the little girl, comatose. Sarah scoops up the girl and takes her pulse. "It's steady," she says. There is a note of hope in her voice.

At this point—immediately after the action—nearly all the tension is gone. The kidnappers are captured, Kristin has been found and it looks as though she'll be all right. And James and Sarah are not at each other's throats any longer. It won't take long for us to have the doctors assure them that Kristin will recover fully and to suggest that she'll need the love and support of both her parents to overcome the psychological effects of her kidnapping. And at that point, James and Sarah can exchange a glance or take each other by the hand and assure the doctors that the little girl will get all the help and love they can give her.

The last question has been answered. End of story.

One other point should be made from this example. Why did we put the child in the laundry basket? Consider what happens to the tension level if the readers see the child when the kidnappers leave the motel. Since the readers know that the kidnappers wouldn't walk out of the motel carrying the corpse of the child, as soon as the child is seen, the big question—whether or not she's still alive—has been answered. And we still have to capture the criminals!

By hiding the child in the laundry (which is also more logical, since the kidnappers wouldn't want anyone to recognize the girl), we delay answering the big question until the last possible moment.

6. *Does the theme of the story foreshadow the solution?* Yes, even a mystery story needs a theme or a central idea. It may be a simple truth, such as "We often fail to see the obvious." Or it may be a more philosophical statement: "Everyone is capable of criminal behavior under certain circumstances."

If your story is well structured, even your theme will help to provide the readers with that satisfying "I should have seen it coming" feeling. That feeling comes about when the theme is related to the solution of the mystery.

Suppose a small elderly man has been murdered. From fingerprints and dental records, he is identified as Carlos, a retired concert pianist who, it now appears, had successfully defrauded the government of millions. When our protagonist goes to the morgue to have a look at the body, we describe it for the readers, from the balding head with the wispy fringe of white hair to the bulbous nose, the overlarge ears, the stubby fingers with nails bitten to the quick, the tiny feet.

Now suppose, somewhere near the beginning of our story, the protagonist hears two characters, Pete and Joe, discussing a local politician who is running for reelection. He claims he lowered the crime rate during his term in office because he vigorously prosecuted criminals. Pete laughs and points out that while the official prosecuted a lot of criminals, he didn't convict one. And just last week, there were three murders reported in the papers.

Joe shakes his head and says that it doesn't matter. The politician is an elected official, a person of authority. If he says the crime rate is down, most people will believe it. Pete is shocked. He doesn't see how people can reject evidence before their eyes simply because the official word contradicts it.

There is our theme.

Now the solution to this mystery depends upon our protagonist realizing that the dead man is *not* Carlos, despite what the records say. The real Carlos has taken off with the money.

At the appropriate time, our protagonist will say, "I should have realized that the records had been switched as soon as I saw those stubby fingers. They were too short to be a concert pianist's."

Our readers should be hitting themselves on the head about that time. We told them right off that official statements aren't necessarily true. We *showed* them the stubby fingers.

And if we want to go one better, we could have the protagonist think about the dead man once or twice as the "poor little man who chewed his fingernails." Notice what happens here. We are focusing attention on the *nails*, but the readers won't visualize fingernails in a vacuum. They'll visualize fingers as well. And when they get to the end of the book and the solution is presented to them, they'll feel as though they've had those fingers right in front of their eyes most of the time and *still* they overlooked the solution!

Notice that it is important to present the theme in such a way that its significance to the solution is not immediately apparent. If the two characters had been talking about falsified documents, for example, the solution would be too obvious.

Nor would it be satisfying to learn that the records had been falsified by the authorities. It would be far better if Carlos had the records switched through his own ingenuity and the authorities were every bit as taken in as our protagonist.

If you are not sure what your theme is, ask yourself what is the point of this story? What did the protagonist learn from it?

Then go back and show the readers that same truth in a different way—one that will not tip them off to the solution. If possible, present that truth early in the book. Then, when the solution is revealed at the end, the readers will experience that satisfying feeling: "I should have known that!"

7. *Is each important part of your story moving toward the climax?* One of the most critical features of the structure of your story is that the plot and all the subplots should steadily move toward the climax.

Let's go back to the example we discussed earlier, in which Kristin, the daughter of James and Sarah, has been kidnapped. Suppose one of our other characters is Sarah's younger sister, Jackie. Jackie was taking care of Kristin at the time of the kidnapping. She is distraught and blames herself for what has happened.

If we watch Jackie during the story and see her distress deepening, it will be a satisfying part of the story. Her problem will be resolved when she learns that Kristin will be all right.

Let's suppose Jackie has a boyfriend, Mitch, and things have been going badly between them of late. Should we watch that, too? It depends.

What if Mitch is one of the kidnappers? Or what if he gave them information—either deliberately or unwittingly—which helped them to pull off the kidnapping? That would certainly be an important part of the story. Mitch thus becomes an important character even if his importance is not apparent until the end of the story, when the connection with the kidnappers is revealed. It is important that the readers see him quarreling with Jackie. He has to be familiar to them (a kind of lesser villain).

But if Mitch and Jackie are quarreling because he went out with Charlene the night Jackie was baby-sitting, their problems don't deserve the importance of being a subplot in this story. Their quarreling isn't leading the readers toward the climax.

Mitch can be there, and he and Jackie can be arguing in the background, but their problems should be given only minimal attention.

STRUCTURAL PROBLEMS TO AVOID

Two structural problems that will bog down any story are (1) apparent repetition of scenes, and (2) long periods with no action.

Scenes may seem repetitious to the readers even when you are presenting new information. Do you really have to make your protagonist go back to the bank six times in this book? Can't he get the same information in other ways? Do you have to have three dinner parties? Could it instead be one dinner party, one theater evening, and a barbecue on the patio?

And if your hero leaps from one roof to another in Chapter 7, that's enough for the whole book. No more leaping on rooftops!

The reason for this is that the reader can easily become confused. As the author you may remember that Lana lost her watch when she went dress shopping on Wednesday and not when she went shopping on Monday or Thursday, but your readers will find it hard to keep that information straight. If the loss of the watch is an important fact, they'll probably have to turn back and reread in order to figure out what happened when.

Some things, of course, have to be repeated. Your character has to go to work five days a week. He or she has to come home every night. But you can still avoid describing these activities in the same way. If you show your heroine coming through the door of her apartment carrying the groceries on one evening, the next evening we might watch her cleaning up after dinner, and the following evening she might be refinishing an end table.

The only justification for having two very similar scenes is that plot is based upon it. For example, it is necessary to reenact an incident in order to prove that the witnesses were mistaken in what they thought they saw. Or a scene may serve to trigger a memory regarding an earlier similar scene.

The other problem to beware of is having long periods when nothing much happens. If your action scenes are clumped together and between them are long stretches without action, it's a good idea to see whether you can't rearrange some of your material.

If that isn't possible, at least try to inject some physical activity into the slow areas. For example, instead of having the detective interview Professor Staley in his study, let them talk outside while the professor chops wood. That way, the readers can at least watch the characters *doing* something instead of merely hearing them talk.

SUMMARY

Structure is the framework that holds your story together and gives it a sense of unity and order. It is created from the sequence of events in the story and the point of view from which they are seen. A good structure serves to get the readers quickly interested in the story, to keep things happening in a way that moves the story to the climax and winds up everything satisfactorily immediately afterward.

13

Maintaining Control of the Story

Beginning mystery writers often feel terribly bewildered by the time they've given some thought to plot, characterization, setting, style, viewpoint, and structure. Writing a mystery begins to seem like a juggling act. How does the author keep track of who said what, which clues have been planted where and why, and what needs explaining now?

It's easy for a mystery to get away from the author. The result is a book that leaves the readers unsatisfied. If you've ever come to the last page of a mystery wondering why on earth Bud left that incriminating diary lying on the kitchen table or how Adam could have guessed that Mattie was Barbara's half-sister, you know the feeling.

How do you, as a mystery author, avoid such problems? Obviously, you must remember everything that has gone into your story in order to be sure that all the loose ends are tied up by the last page. Some experienced authors can do this in their heads. Like the bridge player who remembers afterward who held each of the fifty-two cards and in what sequence they were played, such writers have the gift of being able to visualize the intricate workings of their story as an entity.

Most writers, however, cannot keep track of all the details mentally. What do they do?

KEEPING TRACK OF INFORMATION

The Synopsis or Outline

Most writers use a synopsis or an outline to maintain control of their novel. A good way to do this is to use a loose-leaf binder and begin with a page for each planned chapter. The loose-leaf binder makes it easy to rearrange or add material to your outline without having to redo everything.

Simply list all the important points that are to be covered in each chapter. You can do this in a synopsis form, using complete sentences and filling in pertinent background information, or in an abbreviated outline form, merely using phrases to remind you what is happening. It doesn't matter which form you use. The only thing that is important is which does the job for you. However, for the sake of easier reading through the rest of this chapter, any references to an outline are meant to refer to a synopsis as well.

As you develop your story, you will find yourself adding more and more material to your outline. Whenever you plant a clue or a red herring or you leave something unexplained, make a note on the appropriate page. Then you can easily check later to make certain that everything has been clarified by the end.

As your story begins taking shape, you may find you've acquired a couple of pages of notes on each chapter. No matter. Just don't let your outline get so complex that you can't quickly find the spot where you described the antique goblet or the conversation in which Lynn reveals the true identity of the shopkeeper. If you start getting lost in your outline, it can't help you.

Don't bother putting unimportant details into the outline. Those details that are only there to help the readers visualize the scene—for example, the fact that Kim is wearing a long-sleeved red dress when Roger proposes—can be filled in later. On the other hand, if the detail is vital to the plot—if Kim and Laurel had exchanged coats for the evening when Laurel was shot, and that will indicate that someone is trying to kill Kim—then it should be there.

Maps

You may want to make a map of the area in which your story takes place. This helps keep inconsistencies out of your descriptions. If you have Charley looking out his front window and to the left to see Jerry's place, you don't want to have someone standing on Jerry's porch later, looking down the hill and to the left at Charley's place. Whether Charley's place is to the right or the left may have no importance to your plot, but if the readers catch the inconsistency, it'll hurt your story.

Floor Plans

If a good part of your story takes place inside a house or a particular room, you may want to draw up a floor plan to keep the descriptive details straight. If you mention that there is a coatrack in the hall to the right of the front door, put it in your floor plan. Then you won't forget and tell your readers later that there's a potted palm standing there.

Timetables

A timetable is often a good idea, particularly when you have a lot of things happening in a short period. It is easy to overlook inconsistencies while you are writing.

Suppose Jack drops in at the post office at ten thirty and the postmaster remarks that he hasn't seen Mildred in several days. Later, Mildred mentions that she finally dropped down to the post office to pick up her mail before she went to have her hair done. Somewhere else we tell the readers that Mildred met Olivia for an early lunch around eleven thirty that morning. An astute reader will wonder how well Mildred's hair was done if it was done so quickly!

The problem could easily have been avoided by using a timetable.

A Cast of Characters

Even if you make a character profile for each of your major characters (as suggested in Chapter 4), it's often helpful to have a separate sheet listing every character you mention—no matter how unimportant he or she is—along with a brief description.

Here is where you catch the fact that you've named three minor characters Milly, Tilly, and Gilly. Or that both the shoemaker and the butcher are short and balding and have prominent noses.

Even if these characters play the least important parts in your story, there's no point in taking the chance of confusing the readers by giving your characters names or descriptions that are similar.

Family Trees

If your story deals with complex family relationships or if you make mention of events that occurred to members of the family a long time in the past, you might do well to draw up a family tree. Keep track of dates of birth and death and other vital events which might play a part in your story.

For example, if your protagonist, Miranda, was born in 1960, you might want to mention that her great-grandfather served in the Civil War. That's not impossible. You might even know someone Miranda's age whose great-grandfather fought in the Civil War. But don't get carried away and say that the great-grandfather in your story was killed at Gettysburg unless you want to cope with the fact that both Miranda's mother and grandmother must have been close to fifty when they gave birth.

And if Andy has been married three times and has six children, you may want to be sure of their birthdays so that you won't have your readers distracted by the fact that his youngest son by his first wife is younger than his oldest daughter by his second wife—unless, of course, that's part of the story!

A Miscellaneous Fact Sheet

Even with all these addenda to your outline, you may find that you still have a few details that need to be kept track of but that don't logically belong in any of the aforementioned places. A miscellaneous fact sheet catches such loose tidbits as the fact that it takes thirteen egg whites to make an angel food cake or that the sun sets twenty-eight minutes later in Pittsburgh than it does in Boston.

OTHER USES OF THE OUTLINE

Besides helping you to keep track of what happened when in your story, an outline is a handy tool for controlling various other aspects of the mystery.

Directing Suspicion

In general, it is best to point the bulk of suspicion toward one person at a time. This doesn't mean that several characters cannot be serious suspects at once, but at a given point in the story, the readers ought to feel that one person is the best bet. Why? Let's see what happens if everyone is suspected equally.

Suppose Brent is murdered early in our story. Shortly thereafter, we find out that Amy, Clark, and Deanne each had a motive for killing him. Then we find out that all three of them had access to the weapon. A little later, we find out that all three had the opportunity to commit the murder.

Would you be terribly surprised to learn that most readers won't care who did it? It doesn't seem to make a great deal of difference.

At this point, it might be a good idea to consider the different methods of directing suspicion.

1. *Suspicion created by logic.* In the example just mentioned, Amy, Clark, and Deanne are each logical suspects. They cannot be eliminated on the basis of lacking motive, method, or opportunity.

2. *Suspicion created by emotion.* Suppose we change the situation. Now, though Amy, Clark, and Deanne all had motives for murder and all had access to the weapon, only Amy could have entered Brent's study late at night in order to kill Brent. Amy is the only *logical* suspect. *But*—and this is important—Amy is a likable person. She may have an impish sense of humor or perhaps she's naturally kind and generous.

Do you see what will happen? The readers will feel some conflict: All the suspicion is falling on Amy and they won't want it to be there. Thus, when we show them that Clark—who's properly mean and nasty—had a doubly strong motive for killing Brent, they'll *want* to suspect him, even though it appears that Clark couldn't have entered the study at the time of the murder.

At this point, Clark is the main suspect on the basis of emotional direction. (Notice that Amy has not been eliminated as a suspect. In fact, from a logical standpoint, she's still the only possibility.)

We could make the case against Clark even stronger by finding a way for him to have entered the study, but it is important that we don't do that. In order to understand this, we have to consider the third type of suspicion we want to direct.

3. *Suspicion created by staying ahead of the reader.* We've talked about suspicion created by logic and by emotion. However, particularly in the case of the whodunit, there is a third kind of suspicion created that you must also be careful to control. It comes about because your readers are trying to anticipate what you will do next.

Remember what we said in Chapter 1—that the readers like to feel they have an honest chance to solve the mystery themselves but are invariably disappointed if they do?

This leads to a perverse sense of logic that you, as a mystery author, have to deal with when you are directing suspicion. It goes like this: What the readers want is to be surprised at the end of this story. Therefore, the murderer will have to be someone they don't suspect. And therefore, if someone looks absolutely guilty, he can't possibly be guilty.

Now do you see why we cannot allow Clark to have had an opportunity to enter the study that night? Since he already has a motive and access to the weapon and the readers see him as a villainous personality, we'd be eliminating him as a suspect by making him too obvious!

Thus, as long as we want the reader to seriously suspect Clark, we must insist that it was impossible for him to have done the murder.

A point that needs to be made here is that, simply with the passage of time, the impossible seems to become possible.

To illustrate, let's suppose that we established early in the book that Clark couldn't have entered the study that night. So our protagonist/investigator eliminates Clark as a suspect and does not investigate him further until the next to the last chapter, when an unusually devious method of entry occurs to him.

Will the readers be satisfied? Probably not. By that very perverse logic, because Clark was written off as a suspect for most of the book, they've considered him one. They are not surprised that there was, after all, a way for Clark to have gotten in.

How could we have satisfied them? Well, for one thing, our hero could have kept trying to prove that Clark could have gotten in. Every little while the hero could come up with another idea and each time it will be proved wrong.

Then, when our hero finally figures out a devilishly clever way that Clark could have gotten in and proves that Clark *did* enter the study that night, our readers will experience satisfaction.

And they'll experience even more satisfaction if, when our hero shows that Clark did get in, he also shows that Clark did *not* kill Brent—but he saw who did!

As a side note, you should realize that whenever the hero raises the possibility that Clark did enter the study, the readers—with their perverse reasoning—will be looking for *someone else* to suspect. And that is a good time to raise suspicion against another character—Deanne, for example.

When the hero realizes that his present theory won't work, Clark again becomes a strong suspect in the readers' minds. But now they have a delicious nagging worry: What about Deanne?

In summary, you must at all times be aware of where you are directing suspicion on three different levels:

1. By logic—on the basis of the evidence presented.
2. By emotion—on the basis of which characters appeal or do not appeal to the readers.
3. By reader anticipation—on the basis that the more obvious the suspect is, the less acceptable he is to the readers.

Thus, as you go through the outline of your story, you ought to know which character looks most suspicious to your readers—and why—at any given point. You have to know what your readers are thinking in order to have your story under control.

Controlling Tension Levels

Your outline can also help you to make sure you are keeping up suspense. Every chapter ought to end on a note of unrest or rising tension. The readers have to be left hanging so that they'll go on to the next chapter.

Resist the temptation to have a chapter end when the protagonist goes to sleep. Sleep is a natural relaxation of tension, an end to a day, a pause in living—a perfect place to put a book down! So don't end a chapter with your protagonist curled up in bed unless there's an imminent danger that he or she will be murdered there!

Also, beware of ending a chapter when tension levels are falling for other reasons—for example, just after a minor problem has been resolved. Or right after a humorous incident.

It's very difficult to keep tension rising steadily from the beginning of a book to the end. So your books will almost always have points in them when tension is falling a bit. But those points ought to come in the middle of chapters, not at the ends.

Your outline can also help you to get a sense of where

the major suspenseful events in your story come along. They ought to be spaced in such a manner that on the whole, suspense levels rise to the climax. Thus, exciting things ought to be happening at a faster pace toward the end of the book than at the beginning.

Tension also arises from unanswered questions, and your outline is a handy way to control them. Questions ought to arise at pleasing intervals. They can't be heaped upon the readers all at once, for raising too many questions in a short period tends to make the story confusing.

On the other hand, if tension levels are getting too low at a given point in the story, and there is no exciting action forthcoming, perhaps this is the place to ask the next question.

Controlling the Cast

A glance at your outline will tell you whether or not you have too many characters in a scene. Imagine watching a play in which there are always twenty or so people onstage. Sound confusing? It would be. The same thing happens in fiction when there are too many characters in a scene.

This doesn't mean that you can't have a big party or a large funeral or even a murder at the Super Bowl. But those characters who act and speak during these scenes ought to be involved in the plot. The others—as in a play—ought to be in the background, murmuring. The spotlight should not fall on them.

Each character in a scene must serve a purpose. He or she should convey some information to the readers that the other characters in that scene cannot. If the same information can be conveyed with fewer characters, it is usually better to do so. In general, the fewer the characters, the stronger the scene.

The same principle holds for the whole story. If you've got twelve characters in your book and you could just as well tell the story using only ten, it's a good idea to go with the smaller cast.

Checking the Structure

Some of the structural problems we mentioned in Chapter 12 become obvious with the help of an outline. It's easy to make sure that both protagonist and villain are introduced early and are both onstage as much as possible. We can quickly see whether there are too many similarities between scenes, overly long periods without action, or too much to wrap up after the climax.

AN OUTLINE NEED NOT BE FOLLOWED BLINDLY

An outline should be an aid in putting a story together; it should not be regarded as a restriction. If you are halfway through the writing of your book and you realize that your story would be even more interesting if you made a major change in it, by all means do so. Then check back through your outline and figure out what other changes need to be made to keep your story consistent.

An outline is not a recipe for a story. It is simply a way to keep track of your ideas. Before you begin writing, an outline gives you a sense of direction: You know pretty much where you are headed. But there's no reason why you can't change your plans as you go along. Just change the outline as well. Now it becomes a guide to where you have been. And it will still help you keep the details straight.

SUMMARY

Writing a mystery novel requires keeping track of a great number of details, controlling both tension levels and readers' suspicions at all times, and still telling an interesting story. In order to do all these things at the same time, it is often helpful to make use of certain devices such as plot outlines, maps, floor plans, timetables, casts of characters, family trees, and other pertinent summaries of information.

14

Winding It Up:
Satisfying Endings

We have worked our way through a couple hundred pages of our story. We've plotted and subplotted, structured and styled, developed characters and settings, polished dialogue and planted clues and red herrings along the way. But we haven't finished yet. There is still that crucial part of our story: the ending.

If the ending is right, the story will satisfy. Our readers will experience the excitement of a suspenseful climax and the thrill of sudden revelation. They'll come away with the enjoyment of having been fooled, the pleasure of having seen all the pieces of the puzzle without anticipating the solution. And as they put the book down, they'll feel a sense of unity and of order.

A good ending provides most of the satisfactions mystery readers look for. Therefore, as you come to the closing pages of your story, it is worth considering whether your ending is as good as it can possibly be.

THE BEGINNING OF THE END:
THE CLIMAX

1. *Suspense.* By definition, the climax is that point in the entire story at which suspense is the greatest. For *suspense*, read anxiety. The first question we should ask is whether our

climax is as anxiety-provoking as possible. Does the situation look dark enough for our protagonist? Can we make things any worse? If we can, we probably should. It is best to have the protagonist in a life-or-death situation at this point. If we can't put the protagonist there, can we put another character with whom the reader strongly identifies in serious danger? Remember, the more that is at stake, the higher the suspense level.

2. *Action.* Is the climax filled with action? Or do we have our characters standing around while the hero explains the solution? If there is no action, can we put it in? If the hero confronts the villain, does the villain bow his head and confess? Or does he try to kill the hero? Or take a hostage and run?

What can we do to put as much action as possible into the climax?

3. *Drama.* Is the climax as dramatic as possible? There ought to be a confrontation between the hero and the villain. It is anticlimactic, for example, to find Ardis dead at her own hand and then to be told that she was the one who murdered Beaumont.

Remember that drama arises from conflict, both within and between characters. Does our climax have as much conflict as we can put into it? And remember that we're talking not only about physical conflict, but emotional conflict as well. In fact, if it is not possible to have a lot of action in your climax, you ought to aim for as much drama as you can derive from emotional conflict.

THE SOLUTION

1. *Surprise!* Remember that our readers expect a thrilling sudden revelation at the end of our story. Is the solution to our mystery truly unexpected? In a whodunit, this means that the villain will be someone whom the reader did not consider or whom the reader eliminated as a suspect. Notice that the *reader* must have decided that this person was not the guilty party. It is not always enough to have the protagonist or the authorities fail to suspect the villain.

In the case of other types of mysteries (why was it done or how was it done?), a twist at the end can provide the surprise. We may have suspected from the beginning that Dirk murdered his grandmother, even though her death appeared to have had natural causes. We can still provide the feeling of surprise if we can have our hero come up with an ingenious way to *prove* it was murder.

A surprising revelation at the end is a source of great satisfaction in any kind of story. And it need not occur in the solution of the main problem. Perhaps someone's true identity is revealed, or a heretofore-hidden relationship is discovered. The important thing to remember is that while the revelation should be surprising, it should also be believable. That is, clues must be planted in the story so that the readers can look back and say, "Of course! I should have suspected that!"

2. *Does it fit?* Even though the readers want to be surprised by our ending, they also want to feel that it is a logical solution and that if they had only looked at the facts in the proper light, they would have seen the solution, too.

Suppose at the end of our story we suddenly reveal that Priscilla, the barmaid, murdered wealthy Alexander (because she was secretly married to Alexander's son, Kyle, and they would inherit Alexander's millions). We have to have shown the possibility of a relationship between Priscilla and Kyle. Perhaps Kyle hung around the tavern where Priscilla worked. Or maybe he was reluctant to escort the beautiful daughter of his father's friend to the opera. What if Priscilla once had the audacity to call Kyle at home?

Alexander—and the readers—may have dismissed all this as a temporary infatuation on Kyle's part, but, looking back, his secret marriage to Priscilla will almost seem obvious.

We also have to have shown that Priscilla was a likely murderer. Have we shown her getting angry? Showing contempt for wealthy snobs who don't think she's as good as they? Have we shown how much she wants money?

And we must have made Kyle's part in this believable, too. Did we show that he was afraid to stand up to his father—that he'd be terrified to have his father find out he'd been foolish enough to marry a barmaid? Did we show that Kyle was easily manipulated by a stronger personality?

It is important to realize that we need not point out the *significance* of Priscilla's and Kyle's behavior during the story. It is enough that the readers have seen how they act. Then, when our hero explains at the end how he deduced that Priscilla had persuaded Kyle to marry her secretly—and all the rest, which follows logically—our readers will wonder why they hadn't seen it also.

Everything must fit. As the author, you ought to be able to go back to the text and point to the clues to the solution. In fact, it is often good to have someone in the story refer to them at the end and say, "I should have realized the truth when I saw . . ." or "I should have known as soon as I heard that . . ." This will reinforce the feeling on the part of the readers that all the clues were there for them to see.

3. *Is the ending connected to the beginning?* A good ending leaves the readers with the feeling that it was the only possible ending to the story. If our readers put the book down thinking, "I thought it was going to turn out differently—it *could* have," some of them will feel that they would have liked it better the other way.

One way to avoid the feeling that the ending is arbitrary is to foreshadow it. (We spoke a little about this in Chapters 6 and 12.)

By presenting an idea, a setting or an event in the beginning of the story which is intimately related to the solution, the readers are provided with the feeling of having come full circle. It is so satisfying to the readers to come back to the point from which they started that they will feel that there was no better way to end the story.

TYING UP LOOSE ENDS

1. *Have we answered all the questions?* Here is where your outline comes in handy. Go back over it, making sure every clue is logically accounted for. Did you explain how the second pistol got into the coal chute? And what woke Sophie up in the middle of the night?

There is nothing more disappointing to a mystery reader than coming to the end of the story and discovering that a question has been left unanswered. So, after you've gone through your outline, it is still good to reread your entire manuscript to be sure you haven't forgotten anything.

Whenever it is possible to answer a question without giving away the solution, it is better to answer the question before the climax. That way, we'll avoid having a lot of explanation at the end of the book.

2. *Have we wound up all the subplots?* Remember when we were plotting this story? We were handing out problems to several characters—sometimes more than one problem to a character. Now it's time to go back and make sure we've resolved all those problems.

Does this mean that we have to solve every single problem completely? No. Real life isn't like that. We don't have to design an ending in which everyone lives ecstatically ever after. *But* we've been working hard throughout the book to keep our readers in a state of anxiety over these problems, and those readers won't feel satisfied until we've removed that anxiety.

Thus, the more we've made a problem a concern to the readers—because they identify with the character whose problem it is—the most important it is not to leave the matter unresolved.

If a subplot deals with whether or not our hero, Jon, will win Marsha's heart, we are obligated to let the readers know how things turned out. Either they get together or they don't, but the readers want to *know*.

And if Marsha has a problem—say, a serious illness—we had better resolve it. Because the readers care about Jon and he cares about Marsha, we can't leave her in limbo.

On the other hand, a lesser character, especially one with whom the readers won't identify—perhaps an unpleasant or nasty character—might well be left to deal with his problems.

3. *Has everyone gotten what he or she deserves?* Now that we've wound up the plot and the subplots, we need to ask one more question: Will the readers be satisfied with the way we've resolved everything?

Remember that one of the satisfactions our readers are looking for is that sense of order. In general, they want Good to triumph over Evil. The bad guys should be punished and the good guys rewarded. And no one who is appealing— even a minor character—should be unfairly treated at the end.

Does that mean that the villain can never get away? No, it doesn't. But he can do so only under certain conditions:

1. There is something admirable about the villain.
2. The sense of imminent danger has been removed.
3. The hero is able to be philosophical about the villain's escape.
4. If the readers are left with the idea that hero and villain will probably meet again, they must also feel that next time the hero will win.

Let's discuss these points in a little more detail.

1. *There is something admirable about the villain.* Remember what we said about readers being swayed by their emotions? If your villain is one of those characters who can be classified as morally weak rather than truly evil, and who has an appealing personality, the readers usually won't mind if he or she doesn't end up behind bars. This is the type of person who only kills other villains and then only in self-defense.

And even if the villain is as blackhearted as they come, if he's also fiendishly clever—a master strategist—he can be admired for that. This is the type of villain whom the hero respects. As unlikely as it seems, there can be satisfaction in losing, provided that you feel that you've lost to a truly worthy opponent. This type of story usually requires that the readers feel that hero and villain will probably meet again.

2. *The sense of imminent danger has been removed.* Our readers won't be able to rid themselves of anxiety if we leave the villain lurking nearby, ready to do more dastardly deeds. However, if he's removed from the scene in some other way—say, he flees the country and isn't likely to return soon—the readers feel relatively safe. It's almost as good as having him in prison.

Another situation that works here is one in which the villain is not likely to commit another crime. For example, he or she might be a basically appealing person who was caught in a desperate situation and acted out of impulse or emotion rather than evil motives.

3. *The hero is able to be philosophical about the villain's escape.* What we are really saying here is that the readers will be philosophical about it, for they will adopt the mental attitude of the hero. It helps if there is a bit of poetic justice involved. For example, if a man is so overbearing and rigid that he completely controls every aspect of his adult daughter's life,

finally driving her to kill him, the readers' sympathies will lie with the daughter to the extent that she is appealing and suffers guilt for what has happened. In this case, the victim is also a villain and the villain is also a victim. Strict punishment under the law will not seem satisfying to the readers.

Another example in which it is possible to be philosophical about the villain's escape is that case in which the villain is already being punished by circumstances. The man who mistakenly murdered his own son is already in a prison from which he can never escape.

4. *If the readers are left with the idea that hero and villain will probably meet again, they must also feel that next time the hero will win.* There's no satisfaction in playing against the worthiest of opponents if there is no hope of ever winning. The greatest excitement comes from an even match.

This principle was successfully used in the Sherlock Holmes stories in which Holmes battled Moriarty time after time. (As an interesting side note, when *The Adventure of the Final Problem*, in which Moriarty kills Holmes, was published, readers wept and wore mourning bands in public. So unwilling were they to accept this ending that Doyle was eventually forced to resurrect Holmes.)

The James Bond stories in which Bond continues to match wits with Blofeld are another example of the same type. A single book or story in the series deals with the foiling of the villain's current plot, so the hero meets with a qualified success even though the villain is not captured.

To sum up, a good ending is one that satisfies the readers on several scores. The climax is memorable—full of suspense, action, and drama. Then suddenly—surprisingly—all the questions are answered. The anxiety that has been building steadily through the whole book has disappeared. Everyone has gotten what he or she deserves.

15

Questions Students Most Frequently Ask

BREAKING THE RULES

Q: *This book is full of rules. But I often read good mysteries that don't seem to follow some of those rules. Why shouldn't I ignore them, too?*

A: There's a big difference between breaking a rule effectively and ignoring it.

The rules in this book are not meant to be followed blindly. They—and all those examples on the preceding pages—were presented to make you aware of certain common problems and to help you to avoid them. However, once you understand the problem that the rule is designed to avoid, you can judge for yourself whether or not to follow it in a particular situation.

To illustrate: Suppose you work in a building where many people are constantly using the stairs. It might be a sensible idea to establish the rule: *Keep to the right when using the stairs.* If this rule is obeyed, people going up will never bump into people going down. We've avoided a problem.

But what if it's late at night and you are the only person in the building? Will it do any harm to break the rule? Of course not—because the problem doesn't exist in this situation!

And in another case, what if you are going down the stairs and someone is coming up on the wrong side? If that person refuses to change sides, you had better move to the left. In this case, breaking the rule is the only way to avoid the problem.

As a further illustration, in Chapter 10 we looked at an example in which Jessica returns to the spot where her brother Jed died years ago. She plans to commit suicide there.

But in Chapter 4 we said that it's often a good idea not to give two characters of similar importance the same initials. Even if Jed isn't as important as Jessica in this example, wouldn't it have been better to call him Ted?

Not necessarily. The rule is designed to avoid confusing the readers. But in this case there is little chance of that. Jed is male, Jessica is female. Jed is a short name, Jessica is fairly long. And since Jed died long before this story began, there isn't even much opportunity to confuse him with Jessica.

Furthermore, making the initials the same accomplishes a positive purpose—creating an additional association in the minds of the readers. Jed and Jessica were close while he lived. Jessica still feels a strong emotional bond to him. That is part of the reason why she has chosen the place of his death to be the place of hers. Giving the two of them the same initials is a subtle way of reinforcing the readers' awareness of their closeness.

Again, because we understand why the rule exists, we can see that in this case it is better to break it.

Q: *Sometimes I just can't follow all the rules at once—I have to break one or another. And either way I end up with a problem! Are my stories hopeless? What can I do?*

A: Welcome to real life! Even seasoned professional writers are frequently faced with this situation. It's important to realize that not every story can be constructed without shortcomings.

What do you do? In general, the rule you choose to break should depend upon which situation will result in less reader dissatisfaction. Then, instead of concentrating on the rule you're breaking, concentrate on the problem at hand. Do what you can to minimize it. Compensate. Say you are withholding information for a brief period. This lowers reader identification and causes the readers to feel cheated. What can you do about it?

Can you keep the period of withholding down to an absolute minimum? If it's only for a few paragraphs, the readers may hardly notice. If it's for a longer time than that—say, a page or two—can you distract them? Can you put in more action and drama? Is there any way to change the structure of the story so that you aren't forced to withhold information?

It's only when you understand what the problem is that you can creatively work around it. And face it—sometimes you can "patch a story up" and sometimes you can't.

Even the best mystery writers have half-finished manuscripts lying around—stories that just won't come. Some of them never do get finished. Others lie dormant for months or even years until inspiration finally strikes and the author knows how to make that story right.

SHORT STORIES

Q: *Much of this book seems to be directed toward the writing of a mystery or suspense novel. But what about short stories? Are there any special rules for them?*

A: The rules don't really change. The difference between short stories and novels is more a difference in quantity than in quality.

Thus, you still need to have an interesting character, but

you won't present nearly as much detail about him or her as you would in a novel. Motivation must still be clear.

You'll have as few characters as possible, simply because your readers can't keep a large number of characters straight when they are all introduced within a few pages.

You still need to have an interesting problem for a short story, but it won't be nearly as complex, for you have to resolve it very quickly. You don't have six pages to explain everything at the end of a short story.

You'll do far less subplotting. Very short stories probably won't have a subplot at all. Even longer stories usually won't have more than one. The key, again, is to be able to wind things up quickly.

In general, a short story will have a minimum number of scenes. Again, this is to avoid confusion. You have to allow your readers a little time to orient themselves to each change of scene, and in a short story, you don't have much time.

It is generally a good rule to stick to a single viewpoint in a short story. Again, it takes a little time to establish reader identification and jumping from one viewpoint to another tends to destroy it. Sometimes, of course, a story simply must have more than one viewpoint in order to be told. But if you can rearrange the material so that a single viewpoint can be used, it is almost always the better thing to do.

In contrast to a novel, in which the events may take place over a long time period, a short story is usually concerned with events that happen in a brief time. There are two reasons for this. First, there must be sufficient explanation for reader orientation to a specific time period. Second, the importance of a problem tends to diminish with the passage of time. Thus, if you allow three years to pass before your problem is solved, you'll have to work harder to convince the reader of the importance of the problem.

Q: *Is it better for a beginner to start out writing short stories rather than novels?*

A: That's difficult to say. Some writers write only short stories, other only novels. Still others write both with ease. Neither is clearly the better medium to begin writing in.

It is important to realize that shorter does not necessarily mean easier. In general, short stories need to be more finely crafted than novels. A flaw which detracts from a novel—for example, wordiness—may be fatal to a short story. Thus, a short story may require a great deal of polishing and rewriting before an editor will consider it for publication, so that the amount of time required to bring a twenty-page short story to publishable level may be proportionally much greater than that required for a three-hundred-page novel, particularly for the inexperienced writer.

On the other hand, a beginner may be intimidated by the thought of having to produce a whole novel. The complexity of the plot, the depth of characterization necessary for a novel, and simply the sheer number of words needed can seem overwhelming.

So what is the best thing to do? In general, write in the medium you like to read. If you read short stories, try writing them. If you read only novels, you're probably better off writing them. And don't be put off by the size of the task; break it down into parts. Worry about one chapter at a time.

DEVELOPING IDEAS

Q: *Where do ideas for good stories come from?*

A: From everywhere. From things that happen to you and to people you know. Remember the little girl you saw crying for her mother in the department store? In all probability her mother was nearby, comparing prices of towels or deciding between the green scarf and the blue one. But ask yourself, *what if she weren't?* What if the mother had left the store—and she hadn't done it of her own free will? Who took her? Why? How did they get her to leave the store without arousing anyone's suspicions? And what's going to happen to the little girl?

And the next time the people in the apartment upstairs start moving the furniture around, ask yourself why someone might move furniture. To make the room look nicer? Or to hide something? A spot on the rug? Blood? How did it get there? Or maybe they're covering a loose floorboard. What's under it?

The neighborhood news of who's doing what can be full of story potential.

"Have you heard that Marie's getting married to that fellow she met only a month ago? And he's ten years younger than she!"

He probably loves her, but ask yourself, *what if he doesn't?* Why is he marrying her? Does she have money? Social standing? A relative who'll give him a high-paying job? Or, turn things around. Maybe *she's* marrying him for *his* money. And whoever's got the hidden motives, what kind of lies are being told? What kind of promises are being made?

Some people say—and not without justification—that mystery writers have evil little minds. They're *always* suspicious of people's motives. It may be true, but as long as one doesn't confuse real people in real situations with imaginary people in hypothetical situations, little harm will come of it.

Newspaper accounts, especially the short ones that don't give a lot of factual information, can be fertile sources of ideas. Because the answers *aren't* there, your imagination is free to create a story from a few intriguing facts.

Nonfiction of any sort will give you a lot of colorful information that may eventually find its way into your stories. *Whenever you come across a new piece of information, ask yourself, "How could that cause a problem for someone?"*

When the bats that live in the Carlsbad Caverns leave the caves to migrate to Mexico for the winter, as many as five thousand bats fly out per minute. That's an interesting fact. Such a bat flight could be quite a problem for someone trying to get into a cave.

Why would someone need to get into a cave at a particular time? Perhaps he's stashed a few million dollars worth of bearer bonds in the cave and the authorities are hot on his trail. A cohort has a helicopter standing nearby. If they can just slip across the border, they've got a good chance of getting away. He gets to the mouth of the cave and—*Whoosh!* The migration's just beginning . . .

The one place *not* to look for ideas is in other people's books. Rehashing someone else's ideas is like baking a cake from an instant mix. Anyone could have made that cake. There's nothing special about it because there's nothing of *yourself* in it. Ideally, every story you write will have some ideas and details that you and only you, with your particular ideas and experiences, could have put there.

WRITING HABITS

Q: *I'd love to write. But I have so little time. Is it still possible for me to be a writer?*

A: Do you have an hour a day? One hour a day, three hundred and sixty-five days a year will give you the equivalent of forty-five eight-hour days every year. Surely you can write something in that time! And if you write faithfully, every day, you'll find that you don't need the preparation time to organize your ideas that you need when you only sit down to write once in two weeks.

Don't forget that a good part of writing fiction is done in the head. This means that you can be working on your story while you're mowing the lawn, walking the dog, washing the car, or doing the laundry. Then when you sit down to the typewriter your ideas are ready to be put on paper. The important thing is that you sit down to the typewriter (or the notebook) *regularly*. The length of the session is less important.

Q: *What do you think is the most important thing for a beginner to remember while writing?*

A: Remember to have fun! Write the kind of book you'd love to read. Relax and enjoy. Don't worry a lot while you're writing. The important thing is to get your thoughts on paper. You can polish and rewrite afterward.

This is not to say that you shouldn't strive to write well at all times, even in a first draft. But don't let yourself become paralyzed by the knowledge that what you've written isn't perfect yet. Remember that your subconscious mind is a full partner in the creative process and it won't function if you're uptight.

Get into your character's shoes and *live* your story. If your hero's heart is racing as he enters the abandoned warehouse, your heart should be racing as you write about it.

Feel the excitement! The drama! The suspense!

Enjoy writing your story and your readers will enjoy reading it.

Appendix:
Recommended Reading

The following list of books is by no means a definitive one. It is offered as a sample cross-section of the mystery/suspense field, with examples of various types of stories and techniques. Included are a number of the author's favorites. You'll want to add your own to the list.

Cain, James M. *The Postman Always Rings Twice*. New York: Alfred A. Knopf, 1934.
A fast-moving, violent, and realistic story told from the point of view of the murderer.

Chandler, Raymond. *The Big Sleep*. New York: Alfred A. Knopf, 1939.
A classic example of the hard-boiled detective story.

Christie, Agatha. *The Murder of Roger Ackroyd*. New York: Dodd-Mead, 1926.
Another classic. The skillful handling of viewpoint, upon which the solution rests, is worth studying.

Cross, Amanda. *The James Joyce Murder*. New York: The Macmillan Co., 1967.

A sophisticated mystery with literary overtones. A good example of a woman as sleuth.

> Davis, Mildred. *The Invisible Boarder*. New York: Random House, 1974.

Seemingly ordinary people in an everyday setting, but watch how the author creates a sense of rising horror.

> Doyle, Sir Arthur Conan. *The Hound of the Baskervilles*. (First published in *The Strand Magazine* in 1901. May be found in *The Complete Sherlock Holmes*, published by Doubleday & Co., New York, 1930, and in various other collections.)

Every mystery fan ought to read some Sherlock Holmes stories. The effective use of the narrator/observer viewpoint, strong use of setting and atmosphere, and the emphasis on logic and deduction all contribute to the continuing popularity of this early detective.

> Forsyth, Frederick. *The Odessa File*. New York: The Viking Press, 1972.

A good example of a suspense thriller written in the omniscient viewpoint. A nice surprising revelation at the end.

> Gilman, Dorothy. *The Unexpected Mrs. Pollifax*. New York: Doubleday & Co., 1966.

Worth studying to see how humor and suspense can be successfully blended.

> Hammett, Dashiell. *The Glass Key*. New York: Random House, 1931.

Another classic. One of the early hard-boiled detective stories. Like Chandler, Hammett is regarded as one of the original masters of this type of story.

James, P. D. *An Unsuitable Job for a Woman.* New York: Charles Scribner's Sons, 1972.
A fine example of a woman private detective.

King, Stephen. *Firestarter.* New York: The Viking Press, 1980.
A thrilling chase novel with a touch of the occult. Worth studying to see how suspense and horror mount with every chapter.

Langton, Jane. *The Transcendental Murder.* New York: Harper & Row, 1964. Also published as *The Minuteman Murder.* New York: Dell Publishing Co., 1976.
Worth studying on several counts: the use of historical background in a present-day story, the use of a real place as a setting, scrupulous attention to detail, effective combination of humor and literary flavor.

Lathen, Emma. *Going for the Gold.* New York: Simon & Schuster, 1981.
Here's a series character who uses his specialized background (banking) in solving mysteries.

Levin, Ira. *A Kiss Before Dying.* New York: Simon & Schuster, 1953.
Terrific rising suspense, made more effective by the unusual handling of viewpoint.

McBain, Ed. *So Long As You Both Shall Live.* New York: Random House, Inc., 1976.
A good example of a popular police procedural with series characters.

McCloy, Helen. *Burn This.* New York: Dodd, Mead & Co., 1980.

A fine example of a modern mystery with all the elements of the classic form.

McDonald, Gregory. *Fletch.* New York: Bobb's-Merrill, 1974.

The use of the third-person objective viewpoint is worth careful study, as is the fast pace and the use of humor. And you won't find a more effective hook than the one at the beginning of this book.

MacDonald, John D. *The Green Ripper.* New York: J.B. Lippincott Co., 1979.

A good example of the popular modern hard-boiled detective story.

Macdonald, Ross. *The Goodbye Look.* New York: Alfred A. Knopf, 1969.

Another good popular modern hard-boiled detective story.

MacInnes, Helen. *Agent in Place.* New York: Harcourt Brace Jovanovich, 1976.

A good spy thriller with a strong use of foreign setting.

MacLeod, Charlotte. *The Palace Guard.* Garden City, N.Y.: Doubleday & Co., 1981.

A sophisticated and witty mystery with a nonprofessional female sleuth and a highly entertaining style.

Parker, Robert. *Early Autumn.* New York: Delacorte Press/Seymour Lawrence, 1981.

A modern private eye novel with a difference: a not-so-hard-boiled detective.

Simenon, Georges. *Maigret and the Killer.* New York: Harcourt Brace Jovanovich, 1971.

A good example of a psychological detective story.

> Stout, Rex. *A Family Affair*. New York: The Viking
> Press, 1975.

The modern armchair detective story. Good series characters, careful plotting and planting of clues. This one has an unorthodox revelation at the end.

> Tey, Josephine. *The Daughter of Time*. New York: The
> Macmillan Co., 1951.

A classic. Worth examining to see how suspense can be built even without physical action or the threat of imminent danger.

Index